Waiters in Seminary dining hall -

In appreciation Xmas '44

From Dan Wheeler, Va

Tom Gullatt, Ga.

John Hurt, Jr.

Rt. 1 Baton Rouge, La.

Jim Stertz, St. Louis, Mo.

Miller Jackson, Sumter, S. C.

Joe Conley College Park, Ga.

Joe Alewine Decatur, Ga

Rogers Nelson, Decatur, Ga.

R. Bryan Brown Baton Rouge

Ed Gordon, Va.

Jim Rowles, Maryland

Roger H. Crook, N. C.

Curtis Nelms ala.

Everette Croxton, S. C.

RW Jackson - Ga.

Kimball Johnson, Ga.

Floy Cox, Jr. — S.C. (you've been swell.

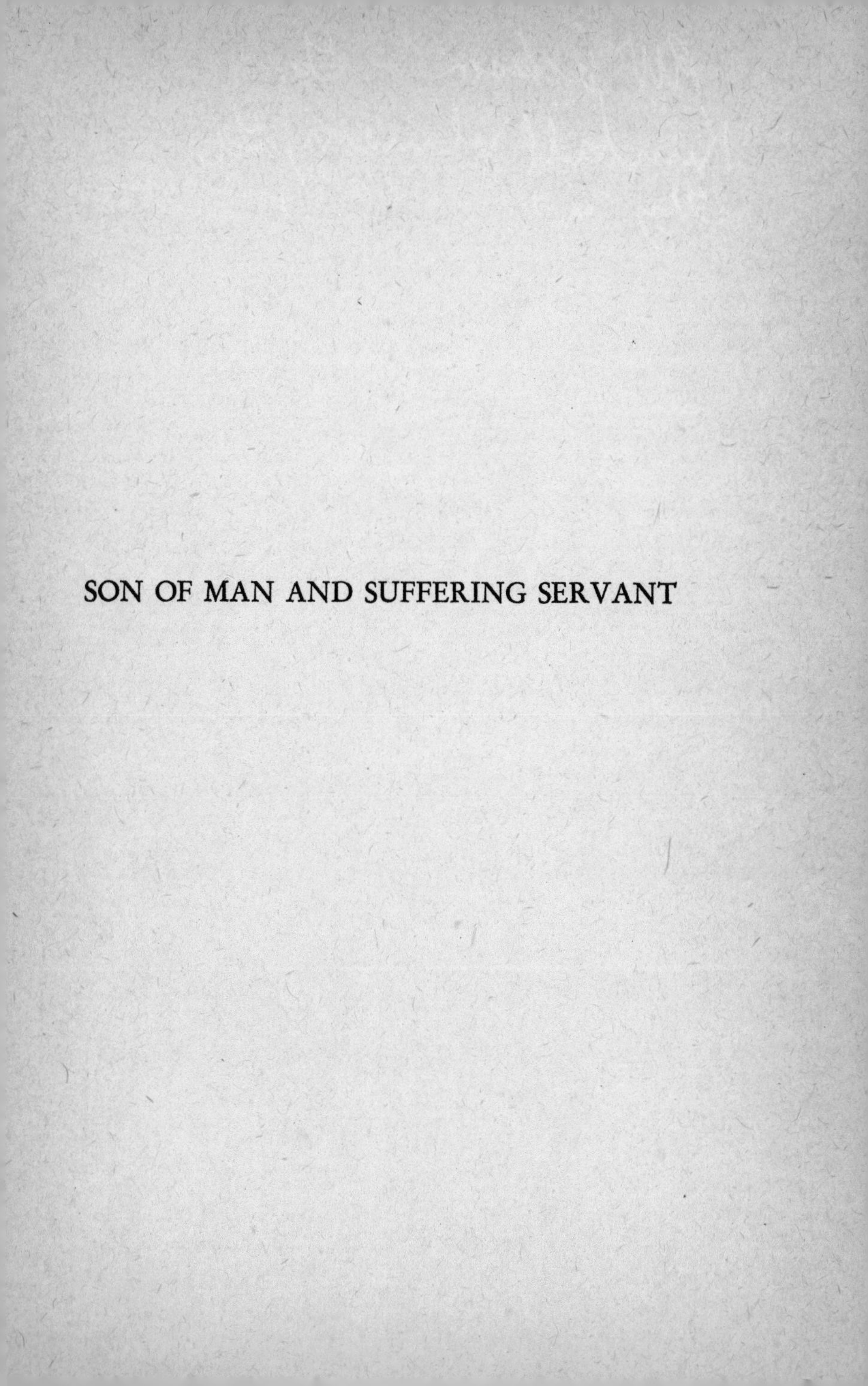

SON OF MAN AND SUFFERING SERVANT

SON OF MAN AND SUFFERING SERVANT

A Historical and Exegetical Study of Synoptic Narratives Revealing the Consciousness of Jesus Concerning His Person and Mission

By

EDWARD A. McDOWELL

Associate Professor of New Testament Interpretation,
Southern Baptist Theological Seminary,
Louisville, Kentucky

To the Memory of
My Father
A Preacher of the Gospel Who Believed with All His Heart That Jesus Was the Son of God

and to

My Mother
Eva Scott McDowell
Who Helped Him Much Through Many Years

CONTENTS

PREFACE

Many minds go into the making of a book. Of this fact I am quite aware as this volume is given to the public. Cheerfully I acknowledge the help that came to me from many minds in its preparation.

To Dr. W. Hersey Davis, my colleague, head of the Department of New Testament Interpretation in the Southern Baptist Theological Seminary, I am deeply indebted for many things, but especially for the inspiration I received from him when he was my teacher. His brilliant exegetical powers may be reflected in all too many instances in the pages that follow. Giving him full credit for the many "leads" in interpretation I have received from him, I shall by no means hold him responsible for the exegesis in this volume. If errors in interpretation have been made, they are chargeable to me. But I wish to emphasize the debt I owe to him and the joy I have in serving as his associate at the Seminary.

In all my work my wife has been an unfailing source of inspiration. Her practical contribution to the preparation of this book was the careful reading of the manuscript twice. Her corrections and suggestions helped much, and her encouragement was all that could be asked. I am grateful to my colleague, Dr. J. B. Weatherspoon, for the encouragement he gave after an examination of the manuscript. I also wish to thank my colleague, Dr. J. Leo Green, for the help he gave in connection with the transliteration of the Hebrew words into English. I am very much indebted to the two Greek Fellows in the Department of New Testament Interpretation in the Seminary, Rev. Henry Turlington and Rev. T. C. Smith, who gave much of their valuable time in helping me check references and quotations. I wish to thank Rev. Roger Crook for his work in making the first typed draft of the manuscript.

Mrs. Ralph Norton typed the manuscript in its final form, and I am very grateful to her for her excellent work.

Permission has been secured for the use of all quotations taken from other books. I am deeply indebted to the publishers for their kindness in allowing me thus to lay their publications under tribute. Due credit has been given in the footnotes to the authors and the publishers of books from which quotations are made. The publishers and the books from which they have allowed me to reproduce excerpts are as follows:

The Clarendon Press, Oxford—*The Book of Enoch,* or *I Enoch,* Translated from the Editor's Ethiopic Text, by R. H. Charles, 1912; *A Critical and Exegetical Commentary on The Book of Daniel,* by R. H. Charles, 1929. (Permission for quotations from these books was handled through the Oxford University Press, New York.)

The Macmillan Company, New York—*The Quest of the Historical Jesus,* by Albert Schweitzer, translated by W. Montgomery, Second English Edition, 1911, Adam and Charles Black, London, publishers; *The Odes and Psalms of Solomon,* Published from the Syriac Version, by J. Rendel Harris, Second Edition, The Cambridge University Press, Cambridge, publishers.

Charles Scribner's Sons, New York—*The Critical and Exegetical Commentary on Deuteronomy,* by R. H. Driver; *Biblical Geography and History,* by Charles Foster Kent, 1924; *The World's Living Religions,* by Robert Ernest Hume, Revised Edition, 1925; *Biblical Commentary on the Prophecies of Isaiah,* by Franz Delitzsch, Vol. II, Translated from the Fourth Edition, 1890, T. and T. Clark, Edinburgh, publishers.

Cornell University Press, Ithaca—*Plato on the Trial and Death of Socrates,* by Lane Cooper.

Longmans, Green and Company, New York—*The Life and Times of Jesus the Messiah,* by Alfred Edersheim, Fifth Edition.

Harper and Brothers, New York—*The Historic Mission of Jesus,* by C. J. Cadoux.

The John C. Winston Company—*The Life and Works of Flavius Josephus,* Whiston's Translation.

I have used the King James Version for quotations from the Bible. This has been modified, however, when it was necessary to bring the English translation more in line with the original. When the King James Version is used, its scheme of punctuation and capitalization is followed. This accounts for the fact that "man" in the title "Son of Man" and "kingdom" in the term "Kingdom of God" are not capitalized when they occur in quotations from the Scriptures. Otherwise the capitals are used. Of course, when quotations are made from other books the punctuation and capitalization, as well as the words of the author, are faithfully reproduced.

This book is the outgrowth of a series of lectures given at the Louisiana Baptist Encampment, Mandeville, Louisiana, several summers ago on the theme, "The Cross in the Life of Jesus." The plan and contents of that series were greatly altered in the writing of the present study, but in sending forth this volume I wish to express to the officials of the Mandeville Encampment and to the thousands of young people who have attended Mandeville for the past six summers my heartfelt gratitude for all they have meant to me.

EDWARD A. McDOWELL

Louisville, Kentucky

INTRODUCTION

A phenomenon of history that forever challenges the student of ancient religions is the messianic expectation of the Jewish people prior to the first century of our era. The prophetic stream that carried this expectation throughout the Old Testament period must be reckoned with in any intelligent study of the religion and history of Israel.

A second phenomenon of history that is inescapable in the search for truth is the messianic consciousness of Jesus Christ. It is now a well-established fact of New Testament scholarship that Jesus Christ conceived himself to be the Messiah of the Jews, though occasionally there is found a scholar who maintains the opposing view. What sort of Messiah Jesus conceived himself to be and how he arrived at the convictions he held concerning himself are questions upon which scholars are by no means agreed. They are questions that have engaged the curiosity and energy of the greatest Bible students through the centuries. They continue to challenge the interest of careful students of the New Testament.

This book is intended as a modest contribution to the long search for the truth of Jesus' consciousness concerning himself and his mission. There is yet much to be said on the question. The subject is receiving considerable attention at the present time. This is undoubtedly due to the renewed interest in Jesus himself. No study of the person of Jesus could ignore the convictions that Jesus held about himself and his mission.

The present interest in the person of Jesus is one of the most hopeful of all signs in our day. It is indicative of a wholesome unrest in New Testament scholarship. There was room for such unrest. The shadow of the old German radical school had fallen across New Testament scholarship in the shape of Form Criticism. Not that all of Form Criticism was bad, but there was enough in even conservative Form Criticism to throw doubt upon the picture of Christ which the Gospels left us. Students could see at once that if the chief contention of the Form Critical School was right, the Jesus of the Gospels must be surrendered, since that which remained of the Gospel records after Form Criticism took away the "accretions" left us with a mutilated picture of Jesus—one that failed to correspond with the old picture which the Gospels had given us. This Jesus was incapable of arousing in men half the devotion which a Peter or a John gave to the Man of Galilee in their time, and he was totally inadequate to the demands of our world, so close to the brink of disaster. It would be interesting to know if any protagonist of the Form Critical theory ever sat down and attempted to forget the old Jesus whom he learned to know in Matthew, Mark, Luke, and John, and then undertook to form in his mind a new picture of Jesus on the basis of what Form Criticism allowed as valid in the Gospel records. It is likely that the effort would be unsuccessful. It is altogether probable that the followers of the Form Critical school who are reverent Christians continue to visualize the Jesus of the traditional Gospels and to give to him their personal loyalty. The Jesus of Form Criticism is impossible as the Saviour of men and the Lord of life.

And so, once again the Jesus of the Gospels strides upon the stage of history to challenge the keenest interest of the ablest thinkers; this, despite all that radical scholarship has done to explain him away; this, despite the disposition of American scholars to be overawed by the hypotheses of German Form Criticism. This refusal of the Jesus of the Gospels to withdraw from the stage of history in spite of the influence of rationalism, humanism, and the impact of scientific thought is one of the comforting and reassuring facts of our troubled times. The fact that the Jesus of the Gospels will not die is in itself evidence of the validity of his claim to be the Lord of life.

The author of this volume cheerfully acknowledges the influence of the present interest of New Testament and theological scholars in the person of Jesus and gladly offers this study as a small contribution to the effort to know who Jesus was and is. It is sent forth in the conviction that a knowledge of Jesus' consciousness concerning himself and his mission is absolutely essential to any appraisal that is made of his person. At this point it is well to consider one of the truly remarkable facts of history: *In the mind of a youthful carpenter in the first century of our era there occurred an extraordinary juncture of two streams of thought having unbelievable significance for all history, one of these streams being the Jewish nation's consciousness of the Messiah, preserved in the teachings of the greater prophets, the other stream being the conviction of Jesus that he himself was the Messiah of Israel.* That these two streams met in the mind of a man is a phenomenon that must always be reckoned with in the effort to understand history. The further fact that this man Jesus in his person and life was the tangible characterization of the fusion of these two streams is a phenomenon even more challenging. An additional fact of inescapable significance is the continuing influence in history of this Jesus whose life projected the fusion of these two streams into the affairs of mankind.

The author entertains the hope that the present study will encourage the acceptance of at least three conclusions of importance: (1) The patterns which Jesus accepted for his character and mission as Messiah coincide with the picture of the Messiah to be found in the higher prophetic stream of the Old Testament. (2) There is a consistency in the character and purpose of Jesus which may be traced from the beginning to the end of his ministry. (3) The consistency of Jesus had its origination in his knowledge of the character of God gained by reason of his unique relationship to God the Father, and in his firm adherence to the principle of redemptive love as seen in the character of the Servant of Jehovah pictured in the latter part of the book of Isaiah.

With reference to the first conclusion named above, it should be said that the messianic pattern of the higher prophetic stream of the Old Testament did not determine the character and the messianic consciousness of Jesus.

Jesus was what he was, and thought of himself as he did primarily because of his unique relationship to God. It was because of this unique relationship to God the Father that there came to him in the first instance the consciousness that he was the Son of God and Messiah of Israel. At the same time Jesus accepted the messianic pattern of the higher prophetic stream of the Old Testament as the revealed will of God and consciously sought to conform his character and mission to this pattern. In conforming himself to this pattern Jesus believed that he was accomplishing the will of God and that he was providing for posterity a solid basis for the validation of his claims to uniqueness.

With respect to the second conclusion, that pertaining to the consistency of Jesus, it should be noted that at this point radical criticism has directed one of its sharpest attacks against Jesus. Views portraying him as inconsistent in character and purpose have been advanced by German scholars from Herman S. Reimarus, who died in 1768, to Albert Schweitzer, who is still living. It is noteworthy that the interpretation of Jesus' attitude toward his death plays an important role in the formulation of these views. Contrary to the conclusions of these scholars, the present study undertakes to show that in the death of Jesus is to be found an important clue to his consistency. At this point the third conclusion mentioned above finds close attachment to the second. The analysis of the temptation experience shows that Jesus identified himself from the beginning with those patterns of character and purpose that were in keeping with the redemptive love of God. Subsequent studies reveal an unwavering devotion to these patterns that made his death inevitable. The death of Jesus was therefore inherent in his character and his purpose. The outlines of his character and purpose are visible in the temptation experience; they remain clear from this point on to the end; they reveal in him a consistency in keeping with the exalted claims he made for himself. This picture of a consistent Jesus is far more satisfying than that which so great a scholar as Albert Schweitzer found in the Gospels.

According to Schweitzer, whose view has had great influence upon New Testament scholarship from the time it was advanced, Jesus expected the sudden coming in of the Kingdom of God with power when he sent out the twelve on the first evangelistic mission described in the tenth chapter of Matthew. Jesus believed, according to this view, that the *Parousia* of the Son of Man and the end of the age would take place before the disciples completed this missionary journey. Proof of this, Schweitzer says, is found in Matthew 10:23. When the Kingdom failed to come in, Jesus decided that the pre-messianic tribulation which was to have come upon all must now be centered upon himself alone. "In the secret of his passion which Jesus reveals to the disciples at Caesarea Philippi the pre-messianic tribulation is for others set aside, abolished, concentrated upon himself alone, and that in the form that they are fulfilled in his own passion and death at Jerusalem. That was the new conviction that dawned upon him. He must suffer for others . . . that the Kingdom might come." [1] According to Schweitzer, Jesus went on the final journey to Jerusalem to precipitate the *Parousia* and the coming in of the Kingdom with power by giving himself in death that the "debt which weighed upon the world" might be discharged. Of course, if this theory is correct, Jesus was mistaken a second time in his interpretation of the will of God. Schweitzer leaves us with a rather pathetic, unsatisfying Jesus, a visionary who could not be consistent because it was not possible for him to know the will of God. It is believed by the author that the picture of Jesus presented by this study is more in keeping with the Gospel picture than Schweitzer's.

For the most part this study shows Jesus leaning heavily upon the Old Testament messianic patterns. There is no question but that the inspiration and background of Jesus' thinking are to be found in the Old Testament and in the traditions and culture of Israel. There is considerable support, however, for the view that he went outside the Old Testament for guidance in his adoption of the title,

---

[1] *The Quest of the Historical Jesus*, translated from the German edition by W. Montgomery, Adam and Charles Black, London, p. 386f. By permission of The Macmillan Company, New York.

"Son of Man." The manner in which he used this title as applying to himself indicates that he must have been familiar with the parables of Enoch, a Pharisaic apocalyptic work that had considerable vogue in the first century. It is probable that this work, as well as the book of Daniel, provided the background of Jesus' use of the title. The present study will show that while he drew upon these sources he stripped the title of its excessive apocalyptic trappings and clothed it with new spiritual meaning. The author believes that in the mouth of Jesus the title is altogether one of dignity and was never used by him, as is generally believed, to suggest his humanity. Considerable attention is given in this study to Jesus' use of the title in the conviction that its use is highly important in determining what Jesus thought concerning himself. It was the name that Jesus deliberately chose for himself and is used by him over and over again. It was highly meaningful to him and was intended by him to suggest to others something of great importance concerning his character.

The method adopted in pursuing this study calls for some comment. Important epochs in the ministry have been chosen, and these have been examined historically and exegetically with a view to discovering what they reveal of the mind of Jesus respecting himself and his mission. These are the Temptation, the Question of the Disciples of John the Baptist About Fasting, the Reply of Jesus to John the Baptist on the Question Concerning the Coming One, the Conversations at Caesarea Philippi, the Last Visit of Jesus to Jerusalem, and the Resurrection. These are the epochs that are most fruitful of evidence of Jesus' consciousness concerning his person and mission. The advantages of this method are great. It preserves the life situation in any given instance and permits a thorough exploration of the mind of Jesus as it functions in an environment that can be studied as a whole. The method also permits the application of the principles of scientific exegesis to a unit of Scripture. The danger is thus avoided of destroying a context by detaching verses or parts of verses from their contexts. The method usually employed in a study of this nature is to compile the utterances and acts of Jesus and organize them under what are conceived to be appropriate headings. This method is of course valuable, but it has the disadvantage of detaching sayings and acts from the life situation in which they originated and the context in which they may be best understood. The method of the present study makes possible a psychological analysis of the words and acts of Jesus because the life situation is preserved. In one instance this method was broadened to include references from other contexts. This was in connection with the discussion of the Conversations at Caesarea Philippi and particularly of the meaning of the use of the title "Son of Man." At this point it was felt that adequate portrayal of the mind of Jesus could be given by bringing into the discussion references in other contexts which could be related to the matter under discussion. In the case of the use of the title "Son of Man" it would have been impossible within the limits of this book to treat every use of the title in its own particular context.

Because it presents its own peculiar problem the Gospel of John has not been utilized, except incidentally in a few references, in this study. In many ways the Fourth Gospel is a book apart. This is by no means to suggest that it is without value in a study of this sort. As a matter of fact, the Fourth Gospel probably contains more matter pertaining to the consciousness of Jesus with respect to himself than all three of the Synoptics together. But this matter often has no parallels in the Synoptics, and it is of such nature that it demands a method of treatment in keeping with the purpose and method of the Fourth Gospel. The fact that John's Gospel is not utilized in this study should enhance rather than decrease the value of the book. Much has been made of the failure of the Synoptics to represent Jesus as making any exalted claims for himself. Scholars have contrasted this alleged lack in the Synoptics with the abundant material in John's Gospel having to do with Jesus' claims as to his Sonship and have concluded that this material was produced later than the period in which the Synoptic Gospels were written, and represents a conscious effort to supply what the Synoptics lacked and not in fact the mind of Jesus. The author of this study believes that the Synoptic Gospels provide a surprisingly large body of material matching the exalted claims which Jesus is represented as making for himself in the Fourth Gospel. Much of this material is dealt with in the following pages.

From what was said in a preceding paragraph it should be clear that the author does not accept the method of the Form Critical School in its treatment of the Gospels. Form Criticism has performed a service in directing attention to the original sources of the Gospels and in pointing out the fact that the present Gospels were formed from sources composed of stories, parables, and collections of sayings which circulated independently and in groups among the early churches. However, Form Criticism became subjective and unscientific when it undertook to delete from the Gospels material which was alleged to have been added to the original stories by the Christian community for purposes of teaching and preaching. In the process of eliminating these "accretions" the Gospels have been mutilated to such an extent that a student despairs of any hope of reconciling the Jesus of the Gospels with the Jesus left us by the Form Critics. We refuse to surrender the Jesus of the Gospels not only because he answers the deepest needs of our hearts, but also because he appeals to reason, which the Jesus of Form Criticism fails to do.

The author accepts B. H. Streeter's four-document hypothesis of the origin of the Synoptics. According to this theory, Mark, a primary source, was used by Matthew and Luke; *Q* or *Quelle* (source), non-Markan portions of Matthew and Luke, mostly sayings, was also a primary source; Matthew used a source peculiar to himself (called *M*), and Luke likewise utilized a source containing matter apparently collected only by himself (denominated *L*). Back of these primary sources, as suggested by Form Criticism, were the many individual stories, parables, and sayings that circulated individually or in groups.

The author gratefully accepts the magnificent work of the great scholars in the field of Textual Criticism and gladly avails himself of the fruit of their labors as represented in the standard critical Greek texts.

When this study was undertaken, and even when the writing of the book was in its initial stages, the author had in mind a series of exegetical studies that would prove that the death of Jesus was the central factor in his character and conduct from the beginning to the end of his ministry. As the investigation developed, however, it was apparent that the better and more scientific method was to explore and reveal the consciousness of Jesus without undue concern as to what it should reveal. This was the attempt that was made. This broadening of the scope of the study resulted in a much richer find. While the investigation yielded a startling variety of concepts as belonging to the consciousness of Jesus concerning himself and his mission, it revealed the fact that in the center of these concepts and always related to them was the concept of the Suffering Servant of Jehovah to which he clung from first to last. The tenacity with which Jesus clung to this concept resulted in his death. It may be said with truthfulness, therefore, that the death of Jesus was central in his character and life from the beginning to the end of his ministry. It is good to see this centrality of his death in the context of his total consciousness concerning his person and mission and in proper relation to the several great concepts that he entertained as to his person. It is hoped that the exploration of the mind of Jesus that follows will vindicate the conviction that the author held when this investigation was begun, namely, that the life and work of Jesus revolve around the Cross and that the Cross is the heart of the gospel.

I

THE DECISION IN THE WILDERNESS

(Mark 1:12-13; Matthew 4:1-11; Luke 4:1-13)

When he came up from the waters of the Jordan, Jesus had heard the voice from heaven saying, "This is my beloved Son, in whom I am well pleased." Hardly had the voice died away when he was drawn irresistibly into the wilderness of Judea to meet the great test of his faith in the truth of the words he had heard.

According to Matthew, Jesus was "led up of the Spirit into the wilderness to be tempted of the devil." Mark states that "the Spirit driveth him into the wilderness," while Luke says, "Jesus, being full of the Holy Spirit, returned from the Jordan, and was led by the Spirit into the wilderness, being forty days tempted of the devil." All three writers agree that it was under the compulsion of the Spirit that Jesus went into the wilderness to meet the tempter.

Why should the Spirit lead Jesus straight into the face of temptation? Does the Spirit of God force temptations upon men? The explanation of the difficult statement is to be found in the broader meaning of the experience called the "temptation" of Jesus. In the interpretation of this experience too much emphasis has been placed upon Satan's enticement of Jesus to sin, the more important aspects of the experience being submerged under this emphasis. The issue was much larger than the victory of Jesus over the temptation to sin. The Greek word for "tempt" here is *peirazō*, a word which means *try* or *test*. The meaning "tempt" belongs to the verb in numerous contexts and need not be excluded here, but it is the more inclusive meaning of *try* or *test* that should be thought of as applying primarily in this context.

The Spirit, then, led Jesus to the facing of a great issue, and the meeting of this issue was for him a supreme trial or testing. The issue was: What sort of Messiah would he be, and what manner of kingdom would he proclaim? The seriousness of the trial and the acuteness of the testing are seen in the use by Mark and Luke of the present participle *peirazomenos* to describe the continuous trial of Jesus through the entire forty days. Mark says: "And he was in the wilderness forty days, being tried by Satan."

Jesus is aware that the issue here involves not himself alone, but also the character of his ministry and the nature of the gospel. He knows that he stands in this crisis as the representative of mankind in the age-long conflict of good and evil. But he also knows that he stands here as the representative of God in this conflict, for if he is truly the Messiah he is not only the deliverer of God's people, he is also God's messenger to men. He is in the character of Moses of old, whose experience in some sense is reproduced here. It was after forty days of fasting on Mount Sinai that Moses received from the hands of Jehovah the tables of the law (Exodus 34:28; Deuteronomy 9:11) and came down from the Mount as the bearer of Jehovah's word to the people. Jesus as the new and greater Moses must descend from his Mount of Trial bearing the Word of God to Israel. But the word that he will bear is the complete word, the fulfilment of the old. When Moses discovered that the people had made a golden calf and that Jehovah purposed to destroy them, he became the great pleader before God on their behalf. "And I fell down before the Lord, as at the first, forty days and forty nights," he recounts, "I did neither eat bread, nor drink water, because of all your sins which ye sinned, in doing wickedly in the sight of the Lord, to provoke him to anger" (Deuteronomy 9:18). Moses sought to make atonement for the people's sin and asked to be "blotted out" of the Lord's book if he would not forgive them (Exodus 32:30-32). The Lord's reply was: "Whosoever hath sinned against me, him will I blot out of my book." Moses could plead for the people but he could not atone for their sins. What of Jesus, the new Moses? He, too, is the representative of the people before God in this trial in the wilderness. He will be able to accomplish what that other Moses could not accomplish: he will be able to make atonement for the sins of the people. Rightful decision of the issue now confronting him will enable him to do this. He, because he is what Moses was not, the Son of God, is invested with authority to choose a way of action that will issue in perfect atonement. And so he stands here indeed as the great representative of the people before God. The issue before him is therefore stupendous.

In other particulars the temptation of Jesus draws into dramatic focus the relationship of Jehovah to Israel. Each temptation suggests an epoch or institution of historical importance in the life of the nation. The temptation to turn stones into bread is met with the scriptural admonition, "Man shall not live by bread alone," the word of Moses in connection with the giving of the manna. The forty years trial of the Israelites in the wilderness, the period in which Israel was being forged into a nation, is thus projected into this other wilderness trial. The temptation to Jesus to cast himself down from the Temple brings this most important institution and its significance into the drama. Satan's offer to give to Jesus the kingdoms of the earth if he would fall down before him and worship him suggests the Davidic kingdom and its glory. In his reply to each proposal of the tempter Jesus goes to Moses for his answer. In each instance he quotes the words of the great lawgiver contained in his farewell address to the people of Israel.

Viewed from another angle, the temptations reflect the three most important elements in the life of the Israelites: subsistence, religion, government. The first temptation involves bread, which is suggestive of physical subsistence, or the economic life of the people. The second introduces the Temple and is therefore suggestive of the religious life of the nation. The third introduces "kingdoms" and is suggestive of government, or the political life of the nation. In these particulars the universal character of the temptation of Jesus is apparent, for subsistence, government, and religion have been elemental in the life of all peoples from the dawn of history.

In examining the temptation in detail Matthew's order will be followed, as his order seems most logical. Mark does not give the story of the temptation in detail. The story as given by Matthew and Luke belongs to *Q*, or the *Logia,* the primary source containing the non-Markan material common to these two Gospels. It belongs, therefore, to the oldest gospel tradition.

The First Temptation

In the Authorized Version the tempter is represented as saying, "If thou be the Son of God, command that these stones be made bread." The verb of the conditional clause is not in the subjunctive mode, however, but the indicative, and the translation must be, "If thou *art* the Son of God." This is what is called a "determined as fulfilled condition," a condition which is so stated that the conclusion is drawn on the basis of that which is assumed to be true. The tempter assumes for the sake of argument that Jesus is the Son of God. It is his wish to insinuate into the mind of Jesus the thought that it is his prerogative as the Son of God to exercise divine power in producing bread from stones. The temptation deeply involves Jesus' messianic consciousness and is designed to compel him to make visible proof of his Messiahship.

Much more is involved in this temptation than the mere satisfaction of Jesus' hunger. This is evident from Jesus' reply, which is, "It is written, Man shall not live by bread alone, but by every word that proceedeth out of the mouth of God." It is necessary to go to the context in Deuteronomy from which the words are taken to understand the import of the reply of Jesus. The passage from which the statement is taken belongs to the farewell address of Moses to the people of Israel. The passage follows:

> And thou shalt remember all the way which the Lord thy God led thee these forty years in the wilderness, to humble thee, and to prove thee, to know what was in thine heart, whether thou wouldest keep his commandments, or no and he humbled thee, and suffered thee to hunger, and fed thee with manna, which thou knewest not, neither did

thy fathers know; that he might make thee know that man doth not live by bread only, but by every word that proceedeth out of the mouth of the Lord doth man live (Deuteronomy 8:2-3).

It will be seen from this passage that the manna was given to the Israelites as a revelation and as a discipline. When they faced starvation in the Wilderness of Sin and longed for the fleshpots of Egypt, the Lord "rained" manna from heaven, thus demonstrating his power to provide other than bread by which his people might live. Hence the Israelites came to see that man doth not live by bread only, but by every word (i.e., creative utterance) that proceedeth out of the mouth of the Lord. By a creative utterance God gave to the people for their subsistence a form of food with which neither they nor their fathers were familiar. Thus in the giving of the manna God was seeking to teach the people his providential care of them. But he was also seeking through the giving of the manna to bring them to *the acceptance of faith as the principle of relationship between himself and them.* They were to gather the manna each day, "every man according to his eating," and none was to be hoarded for the following day except on the day preceding the sabbath, when twice as much was to be gathered (Exodus 16:16-26). Some of the people were guilty of hoarding and some failed to gather a double quantity on the day preceding the sabbath and therefore went searching for it on the sabbath day (Exodus 16:20, 27). Nevertheless the children of Israel subsisted on the manna for forty years (Exodus 16:35).

The experience of the Chosen People in the wilderness is in the mind of Jesus as he is tempted to turn stones into bread. He knows that God provided subsistence for his people in their time of trial. But he also knows that in the thing that God gave them in place of bread it was designed that they should see God's care of them and learn to walk by faith. What of the Messiah of Israel? Shall he not walk by faith? Satan would have him destroy the principle of faith by demonstrating in unmistakable, tangible form the presence of divine powers within him. There is deep subtlety in the suggestion. The satisfaction of his own hunger is the least important of the supposed benefits presented to the mind of Jesus. He saw the satisfaction that he might enjoy as he emerged from the wilderness in possession of indisputable proof that he was the Son of God, having performed a miraculous act that involved the abrogation of natural law. Before him also were the possibilities of success that lay in the hands of a Messiah who could produce bread from stones. Here was a royal road to quick acceptance by the people of his messianic claims—the economic road. Not only would the people be attracted by a wonderworker who could turn stones into bread, they would also be attracted by the bread itself. The transforming of the stones into bread is the core of a much larger idea. The economic life of the people is presented to Jesus as a promising area for the promotion of his messianic claims. Jehovah created an economy for the people to serve them during their forty years' wandering in the wilderness by giving them the manna. Might not the Messiah demonstrate his right to Messiahship by providing an economy for the people now that would liberate the poor from want and assure subsistence for all? Might not the satisfaction of physical needs and the alleviation of hunger and want be justifiable objectives in the promotion of messianic claims? Might they not be made legitimate interests of Messiah's Kingdom? A Messiah who could promise to all freedom from want and a kingdom in which all were assured of economic security might confidently expect instantaneous acceptance by the people.

Jesus rejected the proposal that he violate the laws of nature by transforming stones into bread. Important conclusions follow from the decision.

1. *Jesus established the primacy of faith in man's relationship with God.* The giving of the manna in the wilderness was an exhibition of God's desire that faith be the principle of his relationship with his people. But even with the manna before them the people murmured against God and often rebelled against his will. The manna produced faith only in part therefore; it was powerless to establish faith in finality as the operative principle of relationship between God and his people. Had Jesus fallen before the

temptation to turn stones into bread, he would have risen no higher in the spiritual scale than the Israelties in the Wilderness of Sin. But by his refusal to heed the suggestion of Satan he fulfilled that which the manna aimed at, and became what the nation in the wilderness could not become, the perfect example of faith. His rejection of Satan's overture left him with no tangible evidence of God's existence or providential care and enabled him to accept without qualification the dictum that man "shall live by every word that proceedeth out of the mouth of God." In the case of the Israelites in the desert the "word" was the manna; Jesus was content that the "word" should be nothing with material substance. He fulfilled perfectly the condition that God's Chosen should walk by faith. In this he fulfilled that which Israel was called to attain and could not. His conduct was that of Israel's true Messiah. Because he perfectly fulfilled the demands of faith he established faith in finality as the principle through which God was to deal with man forevermore.

2. *Jesus' rejection of Satan's proposal was a refusal to seize the controls of nature from the hands of God.* His decision revealed his determination not to violate a law of the cosmos by the unnatural manipulation of nature's laws. His renunciation of the exercise of such power was his acceptance of the limitations of the cosmos and his affirmation of the goodness of God as expressed in the orderliness of the natural world. In this Jesus refused to ask a special dispensation for himself and exhibited the moral grandeur and uniqueness of his person. The temptation to lay hold upon the wheel of nature and turn it to his own advantage came to him because of his consciousness of his Sonship; the refusal to put his hands upon the wheel and turn it was the act of the Son of God, confident in his faith that he was the Son. His decision was not a renunciation of Sonship but a confirmation of it. The will and the faith that produced the decision were the will and the faith of one conscious of his power as the Son.

In his victory over this temptation Jesus identified himself completely with the life of mankind. He accepted the limitations of the flesh: weariness, pain, hunger, sorrow. He also accepted death as a necessity for himself since death is common to the life of mankind.

In all of this Jesus preserved the integrity of his manhood. There would not be for him the operation of an unnatural duality in his person. He preserved his mind, body, and soul as the perfect instrument of the incarnation. By the complete identification of himself with humanity he makes it possible for men to understand him and therefore to know God. Had he chosen to live and act as God while clothed in human flesh, men could not have comprehended him and would therefore have failed to come to a knowledge of God through him. In his decision he preserved his saviourhood, for only through one who was truly a man could God save men. The high priest who makes atonement for the people must be "taken from among men."

The Second Temptation

It is not necessary to think that Jesus was actually transported from the scene of the temptation to Jerusalem to experience this temptation. Mark says, "And he was there in the wilderness forty days, tempted of Satan." It was in the realm of thought that "the devil taketh him up into the holy city."

The Temple is the focal point in the interpretation of the second temptation. This institution, the very heart of the religious life of the nation, is the object about which Satan weaves his second appeal to the imagination of Jesus. The proposal is that Jesus cast himself down from a pinnacle of the Temple, relying upon the providential action of God to save him from harm. As in the first temptation, the suggestion is made on the assumption that Jesus is the Son of God. Satan says, "If thou art the Son of God, cast thyself down." The subtle insinuation is that as the Son Jesus may rightfully expect his Father God to suspend natural law in his behalf. The proposal is not, as in the first temptation, that Jesus himself seize the controls of nature, but that he dare to believe that God will operate the controls in an unnatural way to save him from harm and thus demonstrate tangibly his devotion to him as the Son. Satan wishes Jesus to believe that to cast himself from the Temple would be an act of sublime trust, for he enforces his suggestion with reassuring words from an old psalm that tells of the blessings that come to him who finds sanctuary in the Temple. The words brought by the tempter to the mind of Jesus were: "He shall give his angels charge concerning thee: and in their hands they shall bear thee up, lest at any time thou dash thy foot against a stone."

But the significance of the temptation is not to be found primarily in the appeal that Jesus prove his Sonship by causing a suspension of natural law; its central significance lies in the fact that the Temple is the scene of the proposed demonstration. If defiance of natural law had been the chief issue, some other building in Jerusalem might have served just as satisfactorily as the scene of the exhibition. The Temple is the scene of the proposed demonstration because of its significance in the life of Israel. More specifically the Temple occupies the place of importance in this temptation because *it was the symbol of the presence of Jehovah with his people.*

The Temple of Jesus' day was constructed by Herod the Great and was the third temple that had been built. The first was built by Solomon, the second under Zerubbabel after the return from captivity. Herod's Temple preserved in general the design of the Tabernacle. This was true of the other two edifices. The purpose and traditions of the Tabernacle were preserved and perpetuated in the Temple. Tabernacle and Temple are to be thought of as one continuing institution, the purpose of which was to make real to the people the presence of Jehovah. Jehovah's instructions to Moses concerning the erection of the Tabernacle were: "And let them make me a sanctuary; that I may dwell among them" (Exodus 25:8). It was said that when Moses entered the Tabernacle "the cloudy pillar descended, and stood at the door of the tabernacle, and the Lord talked with Moses" (Exodus 33:9). When the work on the Tabernacle was completed, "a cloud covered the tent of the congregation, and the glory of the Lord filled the tabernacle" (Exodus 40:34). When David was considering building the Temple, Nathan was instructed to say to him, "Shalt thou build me an house for me to dwell in? Whereas I have not dwelt in any house since the time that I brought up the children of Israel out of Egypt, even to this day, but have walked in a tent and in a tabernacle" (2 Samuel 7:5f.). When Solomon had finished building the Temple it was said, "the priests could not stand up to minister because of the cloud: for the glory of the Lord had filled the house of the Lord," and Solomon said: "The Lord said that he would dwell in the thick darkness. I have surely built thee an house to dwell in, a settled place for thee to abide in for ever" (1 Kings 8:11ff.).

It would be strange indeed if the Temple, so intimately connected with the *presence of Jehovah* as these references show, did not have an important place in the messianic expectation of the people. It is probable that the Temple in the teaching of the scribes and in the popular mind was to be the scene of the first public manifestation of the Messiah. Edersheim gives a suggestive quotation in this connection from a tractate in the Talmud known as *Yalkut Shimeoni*.[1] It follows:

> It is a tradition from our Rabbis that, in the hour when King Messiah comes, He stands on the roof of the Temple, and proclaims to them, that the hour of their deliverance has come, and that if they believed they would rejoice in the light that had arisen upon them, as it is written (Is. 60:1), "Arise, shine, for thy light is come." This light would be for them alone, as it is written (*ver.* 2), "For darkness shall cover the earth." In that hour also would God take the light of the Messiah and of Israel, and all should walk in the light of the Messiah and of Israel, as it is written (*ver.* 3), "The Gentiles shall come to thy light, and kings to the brightness of thy rising." And the kings of the nations should lick the dust from under the feet of the Messiah, and should all fall on their faces before Him and before Israel, and say: Let us be servants to thee and to Israel.

---

[1] *The Life and Times of Jesus the Messiah*, Vol. II, p. 729. By permission of Longmans, Green and Company, New York, publishers.

Jesus was doubtless acquainted with this tradition. There was also the well-known prophecy of Malachi: "The Lord, whom ye seek, shall suddenly come to his temple, even the messenger of the covenant, whom ye delight in: behold, he shall come, saith the Lord of hosts" (3:1). Malachi was the last of the prophets and this fact of itself would give messianic coloring to this passage which in itself is highly suggestive of the manner and place of the Messiah's appearing.

The second temptation was an appeal to Jesus to conform to the traditional expectation respecting the inauguration of the Messiah's work. The implication in the temptation was that the dramatic appearance suggested would compel instantaneous recognition of his messianic claims. Jesus renounced the traditional pattern of the messianic advent with a quotation of the words of Moses in Deuteronomy 6:16: "Thou shalt not tempt the Lord thy God." The proper rendition of the Hebrew verb here is "test" or "prove" not "tempt." Driver translates Deuteronomy 6:16: "Ye shall not put Jehovah to the proof," and comments, "*Niseh* is a neutral word, and means *test* or *prove* a person, to see whether he will act in a particular way, or whether the character he bears is well established. . . . Men *test,* or *prove,* Jehovah when they act as if doubting whether His promise be true, or whether He is faithful to His revealed character." [2]

The reply of Jesus to Satan sheds additional light on the meaning of the temptation. The full statement of Deuteronomy 6:16 is, "Ye shall not tempt the Lord your God, as ye tempted him in Massah." The statement refers to the incident of the murmuring of the Israelites at Rephidim because of the lack of water and the miraculous provision of water through the striking of the rock by Moses. It is said that Moses "called the name of the place Massah, and Meribah, because of the chiding of the children of Israel, and because they tempted the Lord saying, Is the Lord among us, or not?" (Exodus 17:7.) This question, "Is the Lord among us, or not?" reveals the sense in which

---

[2] *The Critical and Exegetical Commentary on Deuteronomy,* Charles Scribner's Sons, New York, *in loc.* By permission.

the people put Jehovah to the test. Lack of water caused them to doubt his presence among them. This disposition of the people to demand visible manifestation of Jehovah's presence resulted in what Moses described as "tempting" the Lord. In the commandment which Jesus quotes he warns the Israelites against falling again into this sin. Jesus refuses to be lured into the sin into which the Chosen People fell. He perfectly obeys the command: "Ye shall not tempt the Lord your God." He refused to put Jehovah to the test by asking him to manifest his presence by performing a miracle in his behalf. He determined to walk by faith and to fulfill the pattern of conduct which God designed for his Chosen People and which they failed to attain. In this he acted as the true Chosen One, the true Messiah of the Chosen People, Israel.

The victory of Jesus was more complete than the discussion thus far indicates. The renunciation of the Temple as the scene of the inauguration of his messianic work shows the adoption of a method and course of action of great importance in the determination of the character of his ministry. The fixity of the Temple tended to localize Jehovah as the God of the Hebrews, while the Temple ritual and sacrifices constantly tempted the people to interpret their relationship to God in terms of performance of Temple rites and ceremonies. All of this was destructive of the spiritual quality in the religion of Israel and was contrary to the original principle of faith designed by Jehovah as the basis of his relationship with his people. By the time of Jesus the concrete elements in the religion of the Hebrews had virtually triumphed over the spiritual. The Temple, visible symbol of Jehovah's presence, controlled now by men who were true sons of the Israelites who had murmured against Jehovah at Massah, had become in fact the center of a materialistic movement that increased progressively in its demands for tangible manifestation of Jehovah's presence. This movement was the source of the tradition prescribing the miraculous and awe-inspiring inauguration of Messiah's work at the Temple.

In refusing to bow to this tradition Jesus in effect renounced the Temple and prophesied its doom. This is not to say that he did not honor the Temple nor entertain a strong affection for the edifice that he thought of as "the house of prayer," but he recognized that at best both Tabernacle and Temple were but aids and symbols in worship. He knew that in a sense they were concessions on God's part to the incapacity of the people for perfect faith and that the Temple had become in fact an obstruction to spiritual religion. Jesus was faced with the issue of an alliance with institutional religion represented by the Temple and its traditions or a complete renunciation of the Temple and its traditions. There was no middle ground. If he proceeded to Jerusalem and leaped from the pinnacle of the Temple in conformity with the traditional messianic pattern, he would draw to his side the powerful forces of religion. But he saw what this would demand of him—conformity to traditional patterns in the presentation of his claims and the proclamation of his message. In conforming thus to the traditional pattern he would encourage the materialistic movement the Temple had fostered.

Jesus saw another peril in accepting Satan's suggestion. Acceptance of his messianic claims because of a miraculous demonstration at the Temple would be contrary to the principle of faith and in keeping with the materialism of the Israelites when at Massah they asked, "Is the Lord among us or not?" Acceptance of his claims based upon wonderment could not effect transformation of individual and national character. It could not transform because it would be of a piece with the materialism that had done so much to shape the type of character that prevailed.

Faith, therefore, won a second victory in Jesus' rejection of Satan's suggestion. Just as he refused to transform stones into bread as a tangible demonstration of his Sonship, so now he renounces the Temple as necessary to the manifestation of the presence of God. In both decisions he rises above the character of the Chosen People; they demanded bread and received manna, while he demanded nothing, accepting in perfect faith the principle contained in the statement, "Man shall not live by bread alone, but by every word that proceedeth out of the mouth of God." The Israelites inquired, "Is the Lord among us or not?"

and received a Tabernacle as "Jehovah's dwelling place," while Jesus refused to put Jehovah to the test and renounced the Temple as the visible evidence of Jehovah's presence. His decisions forced him to enter upon his messianic work with no proof of authority except the power of the Spirit within him, but because of the decisions he was able to introduce a new and living stream into the life of mankind.

The Third Temptation

Satan brings his final assault against Jesus. He "showeth him all the kingdoms of the world, and the glory of them; and saith unto him, All these things will I give thee, if thou wilt fall down and worship me." It is a dream of world conquest that the tempter brings to the mind of Jesus. There is now no proposal of action on the assumption that Jesus is the Son of God, for no demonstration of miraculous power is involved. The execution of the proposal will require only the natural means that are available through the exercise of human power. Satan assumes that the manipulation of this power is in his hands and that through its control he can present to Jesus the prize of world dominion. The price that he demands is that Jesus fall down and worship him; that is, that he recognize Satan's authority and conform the messianic pattern to Satan's demands.

What is the meaning of the temptation? Does Jesus actually dream of becoming a world ruler? If the temptation is in the nature of such a dream, what is proposed as the practical method of its realization? The only reasonable interpretation of the temptation is that Jesus faces the possibility of making himself the master of the world by re-establishing the Davidic monarchy with himself upon the throne. What other road was open to him if he wished to make himself the master of the "kingdoms of the world"? Was it possible for Satan by a wave of the hand to place them under Jesus' power? Was some great miracle possible that would suddenly place Jesus at the head of all the kingdoms of the earth? No, there was but one road open to him if he wished to accept Satan's proposal—it was the road the world conquerors had traveled, the road of Alexander the Great and Julius Caesar in their march toward conquest of the world. The road always began somewhere, began in some political entity of which the would-be world conqueror had made himself the master. For Alexander the road began in Greece, for Caesar it began in Italy, for Jesus it would begin in Judea. It is not necessary to think that Jesus saw himself as a second Alexander or a conqueror of Caesar's stripe. It is more likely that in the dream Satan caused to pass through his mind he saw himself as a beneficent conqueror, achieving more by influence and political action than by military conquest. The world kingdom that Satan led him to envision was certainly a kingdom of justice and righteousness, for only one of such character could have had any appeal to the mind of Jesus. The subtlety of the temptation would lie in the suggestion that the kingdom proposed would be a kingdom of such character. Its righteous nature would be suggested to the imagination of Jesus as justification for the worldly methods necessary to its establishment.

Is it fantastic to think that this was the nature of the third temptation that came to Jesus? Why should it be? At the time that Jesus was in the wilderness of Judea practically the entire civilized world was ruled by one man, Tiberius Caesar. Three hundred years prior to this time a Macedonian youth, younger than Jesus, had made himself the master of the world in a few brief years. Further, there had been days of glory and conquest in Israel's history. The kingdom of David and Solomon extended from Mount Hermon in the north to the Red Sea in the south, and from the Mediterranean Sea in the west to the Arabian Desert far beyond the Jordan in the east. During the Maccabean era Israel had arisen from the shameful dust of seeming hopeless subjugation under the Syrian rulers to a brief but brilliant existence of national autonomy. Under Alexander Janneus (105-78 B.C.) the kingdom "extended along the Mediterranean coast from Mount Carmel to the borders of Egypt, in central Palestine from upper Galilee to the South Country, and in the east-

Jordan land from east of the Sea of Galilee to the Arnon."[3] If one who had been a shepherd boy could extend the boundaries of Israel from Mount Hermon to the Red Sea, was it fantastic for the Carpenter of Nazareth to dream of reestablishing that kingdom and by means of it making himself the master of the world?

On the side of the dream was the undying hope of the Jews that one day Israel would rule the world. There was also the expectation that Messiah would come as a deliverer to free the nation from the yoke of foreign domination. The hope is seen in the following passage from *The Odes and Psalms of Solomon*, a work dated by J. Rendel Harris in the first century B.C.:

> Behold, O Lord, and raise up to them their king, the Son of David, according to the time which thou seest, O God: and let Him reign over Israel thy servant, and strengthen Him with power that He may humble the sinful rulers: and may purify Jerusalem from the Gentiles who trample her down to destruction, so as to destroy the wicked from my inheritance: and to break their pride like a potter's vessel: to break with a rod of iron all their firmness: to destroy the sinful Gentiles with the word of his mouth: at His rebuke the Gentiles shall flee from before His face: and to confute sinners by the word of their heart: that He may gather together a holy people that shall exult in righteousness: and may judge the tribes of the people whom the Lord His God sanctified: and He shall not any more suffer sin to lodge amongst them; and no more shall dwell amongst them the man that knoweth evil. For he knoweth them that they are all the children of God, and He shall divide them according to their tribes upon the earth: and the sojourner and the foreigner shall not dwell with them: for He will judge the Gentiles and the peoples in the wisdom of His righteousness: and He shall possess a people from among the Gentiles: and they shall serve Him under His yoke: and they shall praise the Lord openly over all the earth: and He shall purify Jerusalem in holiness, as it was of old time: that the Gentiles may come from the ends of the earth to behold His glory: bringing her sons with them as an honorable gift; those who were scattered from her, and to see the glory of the Lord wherewith He hath glorified her: and He the righteous king, taught of God, is over them: and there is no wicked person in His days amongst them, because they are all righteous, and their king is the Lord Messiah: for He will not trust on horse nor on his rider; nor on the bow: nor shall

[3] *Biblical Geography and History*, by Charles Foster Kent, Charles Scribner's Sons, New York, p. 227. By permission.

He multiply to himself of gold and silver for war: nor shall He rely on a multitude in the day of war (17:23-37).[4]

The quotation speaks for itself as a pointed illustration of the intense nationalistic feeling of the Jews and of the nature of the expectation that they held concerning the universal and righteous reign of the Messiah. The wars of the Maccabees, the popularity of the Zealots, and the fatal revolt against Rome that led to the destruction of the Temple in A.D. 70 give additional weight to the evidence that nationalistic feeling was always strong among the Jews and was easily aroused to fanatic pitch by any leader who offered freedom from foreign oppression.

There were the promises of Scripture that seemed to indicate that Jehovah intended to establish a universal kingdom with the throne of David as the seat of government. Jehovah had said to David: "And when thy days be fulfilled, and thou shalt sleep with thy fathers, I will set up thy seed after thee, which shall proceed out of thy bowels, and I will establish his kingdom. He shall build an house for my name, and I will establish the throne of his kingdom for ever. . . . And thine house and thy kingdom shall be established for ever before thee: thy throne shall be established for ever" (2 Samuel 7:12-13, 16). The Lord's promise to Solomon was that if he would be obedient to his statutes, "Then I will establish the throne of thy kingdom upon Israel for ever, as I promised to David thy father, saying, There shall not fail thee a man upon the throne of Israel" (1 Kings 9:5). If these promises pointed only to the establishment of a perpetual throne in Israel, the perpetuity of the throne would suggest the extension of its rule geographically. There were other Scriptures which suggested the worldwide dominion of Israel. Speaking of the time when "the Redeemer shall come to Zion," Isaiah had prophesied: "And the Gentiles shall come to thy light, and kings to the brightness of thy rising" (59:20; 60:3), a prophecy given messianic significance by the rabbis. But clearer than all others in its promise of the universal rule

---

[4] From *The Odes and Psalms of Solomon*, published from the Syriac Version, by J. Rendel Harris, Second Edition, Cambridge University Press, p. 155. By permission of The Macmillan Co., New York.

that was in store for Israel under the Messiah was this prophecy of Daniel:

> I saw in the night visions, and, behold, one like the Son of man came with the clouds of heaven, and came to the Ancient of days, and they brought him near before him. And there was given him dominion, and glory, and a kingdom, that all people, nations, and languages, should serve him: his dominion is an everlasting dominion, which shall not pass away, and his kingdom that which shall not be destroyed (7:13-14).

Jesus was familiar with these prophecies. They and others of like import doubtless flashed through his mind in the course of the forty days' temptation. He could not have escaped knowledge of the popular expectation concerning the national deliverance that was to take place at Messiah's advent. He doubtless reasoned that this popular expectation would enable him to advance kingly claims with comparative ease. Furthermore there was no king who reigned in Judea. Pontius Pilate, despised procurator of Rome, was the ruler in Judea, and Herod Antipas, tetrarch of Galilee, was no descendant of David. Jesus, like every good Jew, knew his family history; he knew himself to be a descendant of David. Circumstances, therefore, favored a *coup* by which he would be proclaimed the legal heir of David and the king of Israel. The throne of David reestablished, the men of Israel would rally to his standard as they had rallied to the standard of David and of Judas Maccabeus. God would surely fight for Israel, surely fight for his Son, Israel's Messiah, as he had never fought for David and Judas Maccabeus. Victory over Rome's legions would be certain. In time, as Israel's power grew, Rome would be compelled to recognize Israel's sovereignty, and the Messiah would become the ruler of the world. Then would begin that glorious reign of righteousness of which Isaiah sang:

> And it shall come to pass in the last days, that the mountain of the Lord's house shall be established in the top of the mountains, and shall be exalted above the hills; and all nations shall flow unto it. And many people shall go and say, Come ye, and let us go up to the mountain of the Lord, to the house of the God of Jacob; and he will teach us of his ways, and we will walk in his paths: for out of

Zion shall go forth the law, and the word of the Lord from Jerusalem. And he shall judge among the nations, and shall rebuke many people: and they shall beat their swords into plowshares, and their spears into pruninghooks: nation shall not lift up sword against nation, neither shall they learn war any more (2:2-4).

These prophecies sharpened the edge of the temptation for Jesus, for not only did he have a feeling of deep reverence for the Scriptures, he was also eagerly searching them for the true patterns of his life and work. What did these prophecies mean? Were they to be interpreted literally, or were they to be thought of as having spiritual fulfilment? The problem may seem simple enough for us now, but it must have appeared to Jesus as quite difficult. To appreciate the issue involved, let us suppose that Jesus had determined that all these prophecies and others like them demanded fulfilment in a literal sense; it would then have been much easier for him to reconcile himself to the course of action suggested to him by Satan, for a literalistic viewpoint might readily make of the kingdom mentioned in the prophecies an earthly political kingdom. The next step from acceptance of the kingdom in this sense would have been the adoption of worldly methods to secure its establishment; the price of this would have been what Satan demanded: compromise with him. But unrighteous methods would have corrupted the kingdom, for means cannot be separated from ends. Satan saw this, and recognizing the inexorable operation of this law, offered Jesus the prize of the kingdoms of the earth for the worship that he would pay to him. But Jesus was also aware of the operation of the law and he knew that no compromise with Satan was possible. His obedience to the voice of the Spirit enabled him to discover the true meaning of the Scriptures and the proper interpretation of the prophecies relating to the Kingdom. For an answer to Satan he went to the Scriptures and quoted the words of Moses, "Thou shalt worship the Lord thy God, and him only shalt thou serve." Thus Jesus renounced the Davidic kingdom in its literalistic aspect even as he had renounced the Temple. In so doing he eschewed politics, earthly government, and force of arms as methods of achieving his purposes. He refused to make any alliance with them for the furtherance of his cause.

The decision of Jesus was a third victory for faith and spiritual religion. Again he had determined to lean upon the intangible, unseen arm of God and stake his all upon the deeper reality and higher validity of the things not made with hands. In his rejection of earthly kingship he had succeeded where the people of Israel had failed. He thereby proved himself to be the Perfect Israelite and the true Messiah, for when the people asked Samuel for a king the word of the Lord to Samuel was: "Hearken unto the people in all that they say unto thee: for they have not rejected thee, but they have rejected me, that I should not reign over them" (1 Samuel 8:7). The Israelites wished to be like the other nations, whereas Jehovah wished them to be unique. They failed in meeting Jehovah's standard for them. They chose to have a visible, earthly king in spite of the warnings of the griefs and tribulations that would come to them when a visible king ruled over them. (See 1 Samuel 8:10-22.) Jesus was familiar with this circumstance in the history of the nation and the troubles that came upon the people by reason of the kingdom and the kingdoms. Doubtless he realized that Jehovah had not receded from his original position respecting an earthly king and his will to be the great invisible King over his people. He saw that the giving of a visible king to the people was a concession to their lack of faith. In renouncing the visible Davidic kingdom, therefore, Jesus fulfilled the ancient wish of Jehovah that his people accept him by faith as their invisible Sovereign. His decision determined the nature of the Kingdom that he would announce as spiritual. It must be, in fact, the Kingdom of *God* because the invisible God was its King. As a spiritual dominion without the trappings of earthly kingdoms, and with the invisible God as its Sovereign, it would be universal in its government and thus fulfil the prophecies of the reign of God over all the earth.

In renouncing the visible throne of David, Jesus won the right to be the true Son of David. His decision made him the spiritual heir of the promises to David concerning the Son that would sit upon his throne. As the spiritual Son of David he is the true Messiah of Israel, the true King of the Jews.

WHAT OF THIS MESSIAH?

It is profitable now to draw some conclusions as a result of this analysis of Jesus' conduct in the wilderness of Judea. What results arising from his great decisions are of the most importance? What is the character of this Messiah Jesus as it comes to light against the background of the victory over Satan? The answers to these questions will appear in the following conclusions:

1. *Jesus established the primacy of faith.* The fact is so important that it bears repeating. Jesus' rejection of all of Satan's proposals is a powerful affirmation of faith as the basic principle of God's relationship with man. Each decision is likewise an acceptance of faith as the operative principle of his own life and work. The primacy of faith is established in his refusal to produce tangible evidence of his Sonship by turning stones into bread, in the renunciation of the Temple as the scene of the inauguration of his messianic work through a miraculous demonstration of the power of God, and in the renunciation of the visible Davidic monarchy as an avenue to world conquest.

The decisions of Jesus are of far-reaching importance in the determination of the nature of his gospel and in the method of its presentation. His own life must be a living demonstration of faith. He must be faith's perfect exemplar. He must not at any time ask God to provide evidence of his existence and providential care that is not available to all men. He may not resort to displays of supernatural power to promote acceptance of his cause. Men must accept him as Messiah, if they accept him at all, not because of "signs," but because of the authority resident in his person. He must be willing to await patiently the quiet growth of the seeds of the gospel in the hearts and minds of men and not resort to methods of the political revolutionary to promote his cause. His character and conduct must be such as to inspire men to have perfect trust in God as loving Father. He must accept the limitations of human flesh, identifying himself completely with the life of mankind, adjusting himself to the natural world as the good creation of his Heavenly Father. In spite of the hardships and suffering that such a course will bring to him, he must yet see and affirm the goodness and love of God.

2. *Jesus chose to identify himself with the highest and best prophetic patterns of the Old Testament.* He accepted the words of Moses as sufficient answers to Satan's proposals and as adequate principles of conduct for himself. In every case his decision indicated his determination to be the perfect Israelite conforming himself to the highest standard of conduct which God sought in his people. If the people received manna in the wilderness as evidence of God's providence, he would ask nothing; if they must have a tabernacle as symbol of his presence, he would renounce the Temple as the scene of a demonstration of God's power in the inauguration of the Messiah's work; if the people demanded a king, he would renounce the visible Davidic monarchy and would proclaim a spiritual kingdom with the invisible God as its Sovereign. In all this he was conforming to the highest prophetic patterns. In his refusal to conform to literalistic interpretations of messianic prophecies, he found his level in the higher prophetic stream of Israel and marked out a course for himself as the Suffering Servant of Jehovah.

3. *Jesus renounced the particularism of Judaism and affirmed the universalism of the higher prophetic stream in Israel. In this he laid the foundation for the finality of Christianity.* The importance of this fact cannot be overemphasized. In it we see reflected the awesome significance of the decisions Jesus was called upon to make in the wilderness. Upon his decisions hung the question as to whether his gospel would be forever yoked to Judaism or be liberated to the higher level of universality. Had he chosen to conform to the popular expectation concerning the Messiah; had he fallen before the temptation to cast himself from the Temple and thus identified himself with the Temple and traditional religion; had he determined to re-establish the Davidic monarchy and make himself its head—had he

done any or all of these things he would have chained his gospel to Judaism in such fashion that it could never have been more than Judaism. His decisions made impossible the forging of a chain that would hold his gospel a prisoner of Judaism. At the same time they did not sever the vital connection between the Israel of old and the new gospel of the Kingdom. They made possible the continuous and unbroken flow of God's redemptive purposes in history through the preservation of a vital nexus between the old and the new. By his victory Jesus gained the right to be the Messiah of the Old Israel and the creator of the New Israel.

Paul was the true interpreter of Christ and the gospel when at the Council of Jerusalem he insisted on freedom for the Gentiles. The victory of Paul there was in keeping with the victory of Jesus over Satan in the wilderness of Judea.

4. *Jesus laid the foundation for the inescapable conflict between himself and the religious leaders of the nation; his decisions therefore made his death inevitable.* The renunciations pertaining to the Temple and the Davidic kingdom, cherished institutions among the religionists and their followers, were bound to bring him in conflict with the religious leaders. His doctrine of spiritual religion was opposed to the accepted religious traditions and practices. It was impossible for Jesus to abide by his decisions in the wilderness and not be treated as a heretic by the religious leaders. The nature of the gospel he would preach and the methods he would employ would make it difficult for the traditionalists to understand him. This of itself would arouse suspicion and opposition. In due time his enemies would understand enough, however, to grasp the truth that if he triumphed they must go down, because the success of that which he advocated must of necessity mean the destruction of their system. This would arouse in them the instinct of self-preservation, and they would seek his destruction that they might survive. In this they would become the tools of Satan and the instruments of evil. The death of Jesus was therefore inevitable from the moment that his victory over Satan was won in the wilderness of

Judea. It was inevitable because in the character exhibited in the victory over Satan perfect goodness and perfect love were projected into the experience of mankind, and these are forever set against evil—between them and evil there can be no compromise. In this crisis Jesus acted in character as the Son of God; as the Son he revealed in his conduct the character of God. From henceforth he will reveal the character of God. God being goodness and love, there is no escape from the inevitable conflict with evil. Jesus will be consistent because his conduct is based in his likeness to God. His consistency will bring him into conflict with evil, but the conflict will bring to light the eternal redemptive purposes of God.

Calvary is the projection of the victory of Jesus in the wilderness of Judea.

II

THE DECLARATION AT NAZARETH

(Luke 4:16-31)

Jesus chose Nazareth as the scene of the first declaration concerning his person and mission. The report of the incident is given by Luke only, though Matthew and Mark describe a visit to Nazareth similar in some respects to the visit recorded by Luke. There are sufficient dissimilarities in the stories to suggest two separate visits, however, and the visit described by Luke will be treated as distinct from that recorded by Matthew and Mark (Matthew 13:54-58; Mark 6:1-6). Luke's narrative was probably derived from his special source *L*.

The incident is of great importance in determining what was in the mind of Jesus with reference to himself and his mission. The incident preserves one of the clearest and most positive identifications made by Jesus of himself. The method by which he employed the Scriptures in this identification enables us to locate the prophetic pattern that was uppermost in his mind as he sought to make known his character and the nature of his work. The declaration made by Jesus on this visit to Nazareth, coming as it did at the beginning of his ministry, may be conceived of as a sort of "inaugural address." It serves therefore not only as a revelation of the mind of Jesus at the time the incident took place, but also as a valuable aid in testing the consistency of Jesus. From the declaration at Nazareth it is possible in making the test to look both backward and forward. We may look backward from Nazareth to determine whether or not the conviction that Jesus reveals there concerning his person and work is consistent with the decisions he made in the wilderness of Judea; we may look forward from Nazareth to compare his conception of his character and work seen in the declaration there with convictions that come to light later on in the ministry.

The value of the Nazareth declaration as evidence of what Jesus thought of himself and his mission is enhanced by the method employed by him in setting forth his claims. He deliberatetly selected the passage from the Scriptures which he wished to read as giving the most accurate description of his character and mission. His reading of the passage that was used by him was not the result of chance. It is said, "And when he had opened the book, *he found the place* where it was written." When the reading was finished he said, "This day is this scripture fulfilled in your ears." It is possible therefore to say with positiveness that Jesus identified himself as the person described by the prophet in the passage that was read. By determining the character of the individual described in this passage it is possible to know with certainty the convictions that Jesus held at the beginning of his ministry as to his person and mission.

The place that Jesus found in the Hebrew roll of Isaiah that was handed to him by the attendant in the synagogue was Isaiah 61:1-2 in our present English Bible, though the quotation as given by Luke seems to include a portion of Isaiah 58:6. Luke's quotation is from the Septuagint, the Greek translation of the Hebrew Bible, and contains some variations from the Hebrew. The variations do not materially affect the meaning of the passage. As given by Luke the passage reads:

> The Spirit of the Lord is upon me, because he hath anointed me to preach the gospel to the poor; he hath sent me to preach deliverance to the captives, and recovering of sight to the blind, to set at liberty them that are bruised, To preach the acceptable year of the Lord.

The Authorized Version follows the Septuagint and inserts after "he hath sent me" the clause "to heal the broken-hearted," which is omitted by Luke. Luke inserts, apparently from Isaiah 58:6, after "recovering of sight to the blind" the clause: "to set at liberty them that are bruised," changing an imperative form "set at liberty" to the infinitive "to set at liberty." Also Luke substitutes in the final sentence of the quotation the verb *kēruxai* for the verb *kalesai.* The former verb means to "herald," to "proclaim," to "preach"; the latter means to "call," to "announce"; so that "to announce the acceptable year of the Lord" becomes "to preach [or herald] the acceptable year of the Lord."

The reasons for the form of the quotation in Luke are not all apparent. There can be but one reasonable explanation for the insertion from Isaiah 58:6, however, namely, that Jesus himself was responsible for it. The purpose of the insertion, which might easily have been made as Jesus read from the roll, will be seen when the passage is examined in detail. The change from the imperative to the infinitive form noted above was necessary in the fitting of the clause from Isaiah 58:6 into the new context. The substitution of the verb *kēruxai* for the verb *kalesai* makes little difference in the meaning of the sentence in which the change takes place. The omission by Luke of the clause "to heal the brokenhearted" is not so readily explained. Its omission does not seem to have any special significance and does not materially alter the meaning of the passage.

The roll from which Jesus read was in Hebrew. It was necessary for the reading to be followed by a free translation of the passage in Aramaic, the language spoken by the Palestinian Jews of Jesus' day. The giving of the sense of the Scriptures in the spoken language was known as the *Targum.* On this occasion Jesus might have given the *Targum* or another might have given it for him.

In the use of this passage as a key to an understanding of the mind of Jesus considerable importance attaches to the identity of the individual therein described. Is he the Servant of Jehovah who appears in the "Servant" passages of the last division of the book of Isaiah? These passages are: 42:1-4, 49:1-6, 50:4-10, and 52:13-53:12. A comparison of these passages with the passage quoted by Jesus in his declaration in the synagogue at Nazareth reveals an unmistakable identity between the "Servant" who appears in them and the individual who speaks in the passage quoted by Jesus in the synagogue at Nazareth. (1) In 61:1-2 (the passage quoted by Jesus) the speaker says, "The Spirit of the Lord Jehovah is upon me." In 42:1 Jehovah is represented as saying, "I have put my spirit upon him." (2) In 61:1 the speaker claims to have an *anointing* of the Lord which is tantamount to his saying that he is Jehovah's chosen or elect one. In 42:1 the Servant is called by Jehovah "mine elect." In 49:1 the Servant says, "Jehovah hath called me from the womb; from the bowels of my mother hath he made mention of my name." (3) In 61:1 the speaker indicates that the purpose of his anointing was that he might *preach*. In 49:2 the Servant claims that Jehovah "hath made my mouth like a sharp sword." In 50:4 he says, "The Lord Jehovah hath given me the tongue of the learned, that I should know how to speak a word in season to him that is weary. (4) In 61:1-2 emphasis is placed upon the ministry of the speaker to those who suffer and to the underprivileged. In the passage just quoted (50:4) the Servant claims to have been given "the tongue of the learned" that he might "know how to speak a word in season to him that is weary." (5) In 61:1-2 the speaker's close affiliation with Jehovah is seen in the claim that the Spirit of the Lord Jehovah is upon him and in the assertion that Jehovah has anointed him. In all the "Servant passages" named above one of the outstanding characteristics of the Servant is his closeness to Jehovah. In 42:1 he is "my servant," "mine elect," of whom Jehovah says, "I have put my spirit upon him." In 49:1 the Servant is said to have been called by Jehovah from the womb, and in the following verse the claim is made, "in the shadow of his hand hath he hid me." In 50:7 the Servant says, "the Lord Jehovah will help me; therefore shall I not be confounded," and in 50:9 he says, "the Lord Jehovah will help me; who is he that shall condemn me?" In 52:13 the promise is made that "my servant shall deal prudently, he shall be exalted and extolled, and be very high."

It is very well established that the person who speaks in the passage quoted by Jesus in the synagogue at Nazareth is the same individual who appears in the "Servant passages." This is the opinion of Delitzsch, who says in his Commentary on Isaiah: "All that the person here speaking says of himself is again met with in the picture of the one unique Servant of Jehovah . . . we consider that the Servant of Jehovah is the speaker here."[5] We may say therefore with considerable confidence that the selection by Jesus of this passage of Scripture as a prophecy of his character and work indicates his conviction that he was the Servant of Jehovah.

The passage will now be examined with a view to discovering the elements in the Servant's character and the features of his work that are viewed by Jesus as prophetic of his own character and work.

I. The Servant's Person

1. *The Servant is imbued with the Spirit of the Lord.* Examination of references in the Old Testament to the possession by individuals of the Spirit of Jehovah reveals three facts of importance concerning the person who is said to have the Spirit of Jehovah upon him: (1) He is intimately associated with Jehovah and speaks and acts as one who is in immediate touch with him. (2) He acts and speaks with the authority of Jehovah. (3) He possesses the gift of prophetic utterance.

The prophets, and some of the judges and kings, were men upon whom the Spirit of Jehovah came. The coming of the Spirit of Jehovah upon an individual was a transforming experience that made him a pliant instrument in the hands of the Lord. Thus, after Samuel anointed Saul he said to him, "The spirit of the Lord will come upon thee, and thou shalt prophesy with them [a company of prophets], and shalt be turned into another man" (1 Samuel 10:6). When the Lord commanded Moses to constitute the seventy elders of Israel he promised, "I will take of the spirit which is upon thee, and will put it upon them; and they shall bear the burden of the people with thee, that thou bear it not thyself alone" (Numbers 11:17).

[5] New Edition, Vol. II, T. & T. Clark, Edinburgh, p. 395 f., comment *in loc.* By permission of Charles Scribner's Sons, New York.

Through the giving of his Spirit to the seventy Jehovah would bestow upon them a measure of the intimacy with him enjoyed by Moses and a portion of the lawgiver's authority. Further light as to the significance of the giving of Jehovah's Spirit at this time is the statement, "the Lord came down in a cloud, and spake unto him, and took of the spirit that was upon him, and gave it unto the seventy elders: and it came to pass, that, when the spirit rested upon them, they prophesied, and did not cease" Numbers 11:25).

Jesus placed himself in the line of the prophets when he applied to himself the statement, "The Spirit of the Lord is upon me." He revealed also his conviction that he was on intimate terms with God and acted and spoke with the authority of God as he inaugurated his work.

2. *The Servant is anointed of the Lord for his work.* The reference to the anointing of the speaker in this passage may well be one of the chief reasons for its selection by Jesus. In his comment on the passage Delitzsch says, "And when he goes on to say, giving the reason of this (that the Spirit of Jehovah was upon him), 'because Jehovah hath anointed me' (*mashaḥ othi,* distinguishing subject from object more emphatically that the form *meshaḥni,*) we have ground for inferring, from the choice of the word, that we have here a reference to the fact that the Servant of Jehovah and the Messiah are one and the same person. Thus, Jesus in the synagogue at Nazareth, after reading the first part of this discourse, closed the book with the words, 'this day is this scripture fulfilled in your ears.' "[6]

The Messiah of Israel was to be in a peculiar sense the Anointed One (Hebrew *mashiah,* Greek *Christos*). The term, "the anointed of the Lord," is frequently found in the Old Testament as applying to the kings of Israel and to priests, but does not occur as descriptive of the expected Messiah, unless its occurrence at Daniel 9:25f. is a reference to the Messiah. However, the appearance of the term as applying to the Messiah in the book of Enoch

---

[6] *Op. cit.,* on Isaiah 61:1, p. 296 f.

(48:10 and 52:4) and in the *The Odes and Psalms of Solomon* (17:36) is evidence that the Messiah was conceived of as the Anointed One. Thus there seems to be a fusion in this passage and in the mind of Jesus of the concept of the Messiah and the Servant of Jehovah. In the consciousness of Jesus the Messiah and the Servant are one. His statement that the Scripture was that day fulfilled in the ears of the Nazarenes reveals his conviction that he was the person in whom the two concepts were fused. In this synthesis we see the result of Jesus' renunciation of the temporal messiahship in his rejection of Satan's proposals in the wilderness of Judea. *As Messiah he would be the Servant of Jehovah.*

II. The Servant's Mission

The task of interpretation is simplified here if we come at once to the focal idea of the remaining portion of the passage read by Jesus in the synagogue at Nazareth. That focal idea is *the design and meaning of the year of Jubilee*. The reference to "the acceptable year of the Lord" in the passage under discussion pertains to the year of Jubilee. Actually the "acceptable year of the Lord" here means the "year of Jehovah's favor," this being the proper translation of the Hebrew term. The contents and tone of the entire passage confirm the view that "the acceptable year of the Lord" refers to the year of Jubilee. In his comment on the clause, "to preach deliverance to the captives" Delitzsch says: "*Deror ḳara* (proclaim release) is the expression used in the Law to indicate the proclamation of freedom (viz., liberation of bondsmen, and return of alienated property in land to the original proprietors) which the year of Jubilee (coming every fiftieth year, after seven sabbatical periods) brought with it; for this reason it is called *shenath haderor* in Ezek. xlvi. 17."[7] The insertion made by Jesus from Isaiah 58:6 into the present passage of the clause "to set at liberty them that are bruised" indicates that Jesus interpreted "the acceptable year of the Lord" as referring to the year of Jubilee, since an im-

[7] *Op. cit.*, on Isaiah 61:1, p. 896 f.

portant feature of the year of Jubilee was the release of slaves.

The other statements concerning the mission of the Servant as given in the passage quoted by Jesus are echoes of the benefits of the year of Jubilee. "To preach the gospel to the poor" is properly "to announce glad tidings to the poor," since *euangelisasthai* could not have meant "to preach the gospel" in the sense in which "to preach the gospel" is understood today. The proclamation of the year of Jubilee would be an announcement of glad tidings to the poor, since it would mean the return of land that once belonged to them or their kindred. "Recovering of sight to the blind" might well refer, as Delitzsch suggests, "to the eyes being open, in contrast with the gloomy darkness of a prison."[8]

What was the reason for the selection by Jesus of the year of Jubilee as a prophetic symbol of his mission? The answer is to be found in the purpose of this institution and the provisions incident to its celebration. These will be found in the twenty-fifth chapter of Leviticus. According to the laws recorded in this chapter the Hebrews were to observe every seventh year as a sabbath year. In this year no planting was to be done and the people were to subsist on that which had been stored the previous year. With the passing of seven sabbath years, or forty-nine years, the year next following, which was the fiftieth, was also to be observed as a sabbath year, so that the land was to go uncultivated two years in succession. The fiftieth year was the year of Jubilee. It was a year of joy and gladness and was to be inaugurated with the sound of trumpet throughout the land. The Jubilee year was always to begin on the great Day of Atonement, the tenth day of the seventh month in the Hebrew calendar.

The law provided that all land would revert to the original owners, or to their nearest of kin, in the year of Jubilee. All Hebrew slaves were to be given their freedom during this year. All things were to be sold in accordance

[8] *Op. cit.*, on Isaiah 61:1, p. 397.

with the number of years from the time of the sale to the year of Jubilee.

What was the significance of the year of Jubilee? (1) It was an everlasting symbol of Jehovah's ownership of the land which had been allotted by him when the Chosen People settled upon it. Its reversion periodically to the descendants of the original owners would constantly remind the people that Jehovah was their king and had given them the land. The year of Jubilee was to serve therefore as a reminder of the kingship of Jehovah. "The land shall not be sold forever: for the land is mine; for ye are strangers and sojourners with me" (Leviticus 25:23). (2) It was designed as an aid to the cultivation of trust in Jehovah. The people were to look to him for sustenance during the two years that the land remained uncultivated (Leviticus 25:20-22). (3) It was a constant reminder to the Hebrews that they were all brothers; they were not to oppress one another by slavery, exhorbitant prices or land grabbing (Leviticus 25:14; 35-43). (4) The inauguration of the year on the great Day of Atonement would encourage in the people a consciousness of their sins as a nation and of the need of national repentance and purification as the great festival year was begun. Thus the people would see that atonement and purification should precede the season of Jubilee, a season of justice, liberation, and rejoicing. (5) The observance was intended to teach the people that joy and happiness belonged to their religion and that a state of blessedness was designed by Jehovah for his people. The provisions connected with observance of the year would teach the people that the path to this state of blessedness was to be found in acknowledgment of the kingship of Jehovah, perfect trust in his providence, obedience to the laws of brotherhood and social justice, and atonement for national and individual sins.

The year of Jubilee embodied great ideals that were never fully realized in the everyday life of the people. But the institution remained as a factor in the law and colored the thinking of the prophets, who continually cried out against the injustices that the year of Jubilee was designed to prevent.

Jesus "re-discovered" the year of Jubilee. In so doing he was true to the higher prophetic strain in the life of the nation. When in his declaration in the synagogue at Nazareth he interpreted the prophecy of Isaiah which he read as applying to him, he was saying in effect that the Lord had commissioned him to proclaim the year of Jubilee. He saw his ministry as fulfilling the intent and design of the year of Jubilee. His mission would be to fulfil the purpose for which the year of Jubilee was instituted, namely, *to teach the kingship of Jehovah, to proclaim the true theocracy—the dominion of God—and to announce the requirements and blessings attendant upon the realization of the divine rule upon the earth.* Jesus conceived of these objectives as being set forth in the proclamation of that which he called the *Kingdom of God.*

The proclamation by Jesus as the Messiah and Servant of Jehovah of the true year of Jubilee would embrace, as the prophecy of Isaiah shows, the preaching of good tidings to the poor, "deliverance to the captives," "recovering of sight to the blind," and the setting at liberty "them that are bruised." The proclamation of the gospel of the Kingdom would comprehend these as objectives to be realized in both the actual and the spiritual sense. The poor, the captives, the blind, the bruised are to be conceived of as human beings to be liberated from injustice and oppression through the beneficent operation of the laws of the Kingdom of God, and in the figurative sense as sinners to be saved from the blight of their sin to the joyous freedom of the Kingdom. Life in the new theocracy would involve the totality of man's being, physical, mental, spiritual. Its design would be the perfect integration of every individual by making possible his proper relationship to God and fellow man, and by conferring upon him physical, mental, and spiritual well-being. It is not necessary to think that Jesus had in mind in the declaration at Nazareth the promulgation of the actual laws regulating the observance of the year of Jubilee. The practical objectives of the preaching of the gospel of the Kingdom as he visualized them are contained in the passage quoted by him in the Nazareth declaration and discussed above. In the realization of these objectives he saw the carrying out of the purpose and spirit of the year of Jubilee. In the year of Jubilee he found a pattern prophetic of the requirements and blessings of the joyous and blessed life in the Kingdom of God. He also saw that the demands that observance of the year of Jubilee made upon the people were fundamental and were therefore appropriate in the proclamation of the Kingdom. These were: absolute trust in God, love of man for man, and repentance and atonement as essential to a state of blessedness.

Jesus "re-discovered" and utilized the concept of the year of Jubilee because he found it lying at the heart of the prophetic stratum in Israel, because it was ideally designed as a prototype of the messianic reign, and because by identification of his mission with it he could show the essential oneness of the purposes of God in history.

III. The Consistency of Jesus

Is the representation made by Jesus of his character and mission in the declaration at Nazareth in keeping with the decisions made by him in the wilderness of Judea? In the victory over Satan Jesus renounced the Davidic monarchy and accepted the spiritual pattern of the Messiah that he found in the higher prophetic strain of the Old Testament. In his declaration at Nazareth he represents himself as the Servant of Jehovah and Messiah who would bring to fulfilment in the proclamation of the Kingdom of God the ideals and purposes of the year of Jubilee. This representation is faithful in every respect to the decisions made in the wilderness. The portrayal of the Messiah's character here is an accurate reflection of affirmations made by him in the temptation experience. The Messiah who presents himself to the people of Nazareth is the same Messiah who refused to turn stones into bread, who renounced the Temple as the scene of the inauguration of his work, who renounced the Davidic monarchy and refused to compromise with Satan in order to possess the kingdoms of the earth. Jesus comes to Nazareth not as a wonderworker, nor as a leader of a liberating army; he comes as he had emerged from the wilderness of Judea—the Servant of Jehovah.

If there is one characteristic which seems to be missing in the Messiah whom we see in the declaration at Nazareth up to this point, it is the universalism seen so unmistakably in the thinking of the Person who won the victory over Satan in the wilderness. This apparent deficiency is adequately supplied in the discussion by Jesus which follows the reading of the passage from the roll of Isaiah. It is significant that the emphasis made by him in this discussion upon the universal nature of his mission was that which aroused the wrath of his hearers and led to his expulsion from the synagogue. At the beginning of his remarks, and even after he made the claim, "This day is this scripture fulfilled in your ears," the people "wondered at the gracious words which proceeded out of his mouth." It is unlikely that they understood the full import of his words or that they grasped the significance of his claim to be the Servant of Jehovah proclaiming the true year of Jubilee. They were charmed by his words and spellbound by his personality, and they wondered how it was possible for the man who was speaking to be the son of Joseph the carpenter. It was when he revealed that he had divined their eagerness that he perform a "sign" such as he was reported to have worked in Capernaum, and indicated his determination not to satisfy their curiosity and skepticism that their ire began to rise. It was when the significance of his explanation of his refusal to perform a "sign" dawned upon them that they were filled with wrath and expelled him with violence from the city.

It was the parallel that Jesus drew between his ministry and the ministries of Elijah and Elisha that enraged the Nazarenes. It was in the drawing of this parallel that Jesus revealed the same universalism that he had affirmed in his decisions in the wilderness. Jesus told how there were many widows in Israel in the days of Elijah when "the heaven was shut up three years and six months, when great famine was throughout all the land," and how the prophet went outside the land of Israel to minister to a widow of Sidon. He also told how there were many lepers in Israel in the time of Elisha, but that Elisha cleansed none of these but that he did cleanse a foreigner, Naaman the Syrian. It was when the Nazarenes "heard these things" that they "were filled with wrath, And rose up, and thrust him out of the city." What was it in Jesus' words that aroused the people of his home city to such anger and violence? Doubtless they resented the implication that he was a prophet in a class with Elijah and Elisha. It is likely that they felt the sting of the suggestion that their spiritual dulness was akin to that manifested by their ancestors in their failure to recognize the worth of their great prophets. But the chief cause of their anger was the emphasis placed by Jesus on the ministries of these two prophets to persons outside Israel, and the unmistakable implication that the Gentiles would share in the blessings of his own ministry.

The renunciation of particularism and the affirmation of universalism that characterized the victory of Jesus over Satan in the wilderness is thus re-enforced in the declaration in the synagogue at Nazareth. As the Servant of Jehovah Jesus looks beyond the bounds of Israel and sees the wide world as his field of service. This is in keeping with certain prophecies that had been made concerning the Servant. One of these, a "Servant passage," reads: "Behold my servant, whom I uphold; mine elect, in whom my soul delighteth; I have put my spirit upon him: he shall bring forth judgment to the Gentiles . . . . the isles shall wait for his law" (Isaiah 42:1, 4). Another of these "Servant passages" in which the universal note is even more pointed is: "And now saith Jehovah that formed me from the womb to be his servant, to bring Jacob again to him, Though Israel be not gathered, yet shall I be glorious in the eyes of Jehovah, and my God shall be my strength. And he said, It is a light thing that thou shouldest be my servant to raise up the tribes of Jacob, and to restore the preserved of Israel: I will also give thee for a light to the Gentiles, that thou mayest be my salvation unto the end of the earth" (Isaiah 49:5-6).

No doubt Jesus had meditated upon the meaning of these great passages and grasped their prophetic significance for his mission. It is most probable that they are reflected in the unmistakable emphasis upon the universal aspects of his work seen in the declaration at Nazareth.

Jesus was probably not surprised at the refusal of the Nazarenes to accept him. His remark, "Verily I say unto you, No prophet is accepted in his own country," was made before there was a move to eject him from the synagogue. He had foreseen that the decisions he had made would drive him straight into the face of opposition and even mistreatment. He was prepared to be the *Suffering* Servant. He knew that Isaiah had spoken other words concerning the Servant, words like these:

> I gave my back to the smiters, and my cheeks to them that plucked off the hair: I hid not my face from shame and spitting (50:6).

And these:

> He is despised and rejected of men; a man of sorrows, and acquainted with grief: and we hid as it were our faces from him; he was despised, and we esteemed him not (53:3).

The inevitable conflict foreshadowed by the decisions in the wilderness had begun. Rejected by his own home folk, Jesus departed in sorrow from Nazareth, but he went with the conviction still that he was the Servant of Jehovah. He may well have repeated to himself the words put by Isaiah into the mouth of the Servant in answer to mistreatment and abuse: "For the Lord Jehovah will help me; therefore shall I not be confounded: therefore have I set my face like a flint, and I know that I shall not be ashamed" (50:7).

III

JESUS AND JOHN THE BAPTIST

Jesus and John the Baptist did not think alike in all things. Jesus himself admitted a contrast between himself and his forerunner in his statement, "John came neither eating nor drinking. . . . The Son of man came eating and drinking" (Matthew 11:8f.). The divergencies in the thinking of the two men produced conflicts on two separate occasions that reveal in sharp outline ideas that Jesus held concerning himself and his mission. These conflicts are seen in two questions that were put to Jesus, the one by the disciples of John, the other by John himself.

The question put to Jesus by the disciples of John was: "Why do we and the Pharisees fast oft, but thy disciples fast not?" (Matthew 9:14). In his reply to this question Jesus referred to himself as "the Bridegroom." The application of this appellation to himself, together with his other remarks on this occasion, provide valuable data in the quest for the mind of Jesus concerning himself and his mission.

The question that John himself asked of Jesus was: "Art thou he that should come, or do we look for another?" (Matthew 11:3.) The question literally rendered is: "Art thou the Coming One (*ho erchomenos*), or shall we keep on expecting another?" This is a question that specifically involves Jesus' conception of his person. His reply, if it is any reply at all, must reveal something of his consciousness concerning himself. It should be considered very important, therefore, for the purposes of this study.

The value of the replies of Jesus to these questions may be seen by consideration of these facts: (1) They reveal basic differences in the thinking of Jesus and John, as has been suggested. The preservation of this evidence of conflict between the two men is attestation of the genuineness of the narratives involved. The authors of the Gospels would hardly have preserved them for the purpose of perpetuating an embarrassing cleavage between Jesus and his forerunner. The fidelity of the authors of the Synoptics to the primitive sources is illustrated in their preservation. (2) They represent very deep and positive convictions on the part of Jesus. Assuredly it must have been a source of grief to Jesus that he should be compelled to set his ideas over in contrast against those of his forerunner. It was only the stern necessity of deep conviction and loyalty to truth that compelled him to do so. (3) The replies of Jesus possess the inherent validity of that which springs spontaneously from a life situation. The replies are not studied utterances but spontaneous expressions of the mind of Jesus, struck out like sparks from a glowing iron upon an anvil. (4) It is possible to determine approximately the point chronologically in the ministry of Jesus when the statements were made. Of necessity they came during the lifetime of John. This places them in the first year of the public ministry of Jesus. However, the fact that they reveal conflict between Jesus and John demands that they be located far enough along in the ministry to allow for sufficient activity and teaching on the part of Jesus to produce grounds for comparison and contrast. The questions were put to Jesus probably during the first six months of the great Galilean ministry, several months after his appearance in the synagogue at Nazareth. They came at a time sufficiently advanced, therefore, to reveal the mature conviction of Jesus in the light of experience. It is possible to study the revelation that he makes of his thinking in these replies against the background of both the temptation and the declaration at Nazareth with a view to determining if these expressions are in harmony with the prior decisions and utterances.

I. Jesus as the Bridegroom

(Mark 2:18-22; Matthew 9:14-17; Luke 5:33-39)

The source of this narrative is Mark. Matthew and Luke follow Mark.

In Matthew's account it was the disciples of John who propounded to Jesus the question, "Why do we and the Pharisees fast oft, but thy disciples fast not?" According to Mark the Pharisees joined with the disciples of John in putting the question to Jesus. Luke represents the Pharisees and "their scribes" as asking the question (5:30, 33). It is clear that the question was asked by both John's disciples and the Pharisees.

The reply of Jesus is, according to Matthew, "Can the children of the bridechamber mourn, as long as the bridegroom is with them? But the days will come, when the bridegroom will be taken away from them, and then shall they fast." There follows the parable concerning the sewing of a new patch on an old garment and the putting of new wine into old bottles. Mark and Luke have in place of "mourn" the word "fast" in the reply of Jesus. Mark's version reads, "Can the children of the bridechamber fast, while the bridegroom is with them?" Matthew's interpretation of fasting as mourning is interesting.

The Jewish marriage week is used by Jesus in the reply that he gives to his questioners to illustrate important truths concerning his person and work. It is necessary therefore to know something of the nature of this institution in order to appreciate more fully the meaning of Jesus' teaching. In describing the institution Edersheim says: "By universal consent and according to Rabbinic law, this was to be a time of unmixed festivity. Even on the Day of Atonement a bride was allowed to relax one of the ordinances of that strictest fast. During the marriage week all mourning was to be suspended—even the obligation of the prescribed daily prayers ceased. It was regarded as a religious duty to gladden the bride and bridegroom."[1] He goes on to say that a Talmudic ordinance "absolved 'the friends of the bridegroom,' and all the 'sons of the bridechamber,' even from the duty of dwelling in booths (at the Feast of Tabernacles)."[2]

Jesus' reference to himself as the "Bridegroom" and

---

[1] *Life and Times of Jesus the Messiah,* Vol. I, Longmans, Green and Company, New York, p. 663.

[2] *Ibid.*

his allusion to his disciples as "sons of the bridechamber" are quite suggestive in the light of this explanation. The duty of the "sons of the bridechamber" was a joyous one, that of serving the bridegroom, preparing for the wedding festivities and acting generally in the bridegroom's interest. The climax of the Jewish marriage week came when the bridegroom, accompanied by the "sons of the bridechamber," went to the home of the bride and conducted her with her attendants and friends to his own home, or the home of his parents. The wedding feast followed and the bridegroom took the bride as his wife.

What is revealed in this reply of Jesus as to the opinions he held concerning his person and his mission?

1. *The declaration distinguishes the ministry of Jesus from Pharisaism.* The disciples of John the Baptist had joined with the Pharisees in propounding the question which brought forth from Jesus the comparison of his ministry to a marriage week. This and the plain statement of Mark that John's disciples and the Pharisees "were fasting" is evidence that John the Baptist did not break with traditional religion, that is, Pharisaism. The ministry of the Baptist was thus wrought out within the framework of the prevailing Jewish religious system. When the issue of conformity was presented to Jesus in this question that came to him through John's disciples he found it necessary to accept the issue and declare his independence of Pharisaism. The declaration involved conflict with John, but in this conflict is brought to light important elements in Jesus' conception of his character and mission. He reveals himself in the role of Bridegroom in the midst of the marriage week; in this his character and conduct could not be in harmony with the prevailing religious system—Pharisaism.

In the matter of fasting, the point at which John's disciples and the Pharisees made issue with Jesus, the formalism of the religious system which Jesus renounced is clearly seen. According to Edersheim, "Rabbinism gave an altogether external aspect to fasting." This author states that fasting, in the view of the Jews, "was the readiest means of turning aside any threatening calamity, such as drought, pestilence, or national danger. This, *ex opere operato:* because fasting was self-punishment and mortification, not because a fast meant mourning (for sin, not for its punishment), and hence indicated humiliation, acknowledgment of sin, and repentance. The second and fifth days of the week (Monday and Thursday) were those appointed for public fasts, because Moses was supposed to have gone up the Mount for the second Tables of the Law on a Thursday, and to have returned on a Monday. . . . Now there were such painful minutiae of externalism, as those which ruled how, on a less strict fast, a person might wash and anoint; while on the strictest fast, it was prohibited even to salute one another.''[3]

The nonspiritual quality of a religion which fostered such formalistic practices is apparent. It is understandable how such a religion was a burden to the people and how it was devoid of the elements of joyousness and spontaneity. It is also understandable why Matthew represents Jesus as asking in response to the question of John's disciples, ''Can the children of the bridechamber *mourn,* as long as the bridegroom is with them?'' The reply of Jesus was at once an indictment of the Jewish religion of his day and a revelation of that joyousness and spontaneity in his gospel that helped to set it in such marked contrast with Pharisaism.

Jesus was a bridegroom, his disciples were ''sons of the bridechamber,'' his ministry a happy marriage week! How could there be fasting, how could there be mourning? The Bridegroom was preparing to take a bride, and the ''sons of the bridechamber'' were about the happy business of helping to make all things ready for the wedding feast! This was no season to introduce customs that were foreign to the spirit and purpose of a marriage week.

Thus did Jesus renounce Pharisaism as incompatible with the spirit and character of his gospel. Thus did he indicate that there could be no fusion of his gospel with formal religion. The phraseology chosen to convey the truth concerning the character of his gospel was peculiarly appropri-

[3] *Op. cit.,* p. 662 f.

ate in a reply to John the Baptist, for John had himself used the figure of the Bridegroom in reference to Jesus. He had said, "He that hath the bride is the bridegroom: but the friend of the bridegroom, which standeth and heareth him, rejoiceth greatly because of the bridegroom's voice; this my joy therefore is fulfilled" (John 3:29). Apparently Jesus was familiar with these words of his Herald, and it appears as if he tactfully accepted John's designation of himself as the Bridegroom and reminding the Baptist of his figure seemed to say, "Apply your own chosen parable to the situation—if I am the Bridegroom, as you say, how can the 'sons of the bridechamber' mourn any more than you 'the friend of the bridegroom' mourn?—should they not rather rejoice, as you the 'friend of the bridegroom' rejoice?"

Jesus enforces his teaching concerning the divergence between his gospel and Pharisaism with the use of the parables of the new patch on an old garment and the putting of new wine into old wineskins. By the use of these parables Jesus shows the impossibility of forcing the new dispensation of the gospel into the framework of the old order of Pharisaism. The new cloth and the new wine are symbols of the new order of the Kingdom of God; the old garment and the old bottles (wineskins) represent the old order of formal Pharisaic religion. The new dispensation of the Kingdom demands a new mode of administration; it would be impossible to attach the new (and unshrunk) cloth of the Kingdom to the old garment of traditionalism; if the attempt were made the attachment would be only superficial, since the character of the new cloth and that of the old garment are fundamentally different; hence in time a "rent" would be made by the shrinking of the new cloth. Likewise the new wine that is the Kingdom must not be poured into the old wineskins of Pharisaism, because the character of new (unfermented) wine demands new (elastic) wineskins. To attempt to express the message of the Kingdom by means of the forms of Pharisaism would be as unwise as to pour unfermented wine into old bottles, since the inevitable result would be the bursting of the old bottles in the process of the new wine's fermentation.

Thus Jesus emphasizes the incompatibility between the gospel of the Kingdom and formal religion—whether that religion be Pharisaism or present-day churchism. In the gospel of the Kingdom there is a *newness,* a *vitality,* a *spirit* to which the forms of institutionalized religion are inappropriate. The gospel of the Kingdom demands modes of expression that are in keeping with the character of the gospel.

The reply of Jesus to the question of John's disciples is a vigorous reaffirmation of decisions made in the wilderness and of patterns revealed in the declaration in the synagogue at Nazareth. We see in the reply concerning fasting a practical demonstration of the renunciation in the wilderness of the Temple and its institutions as necessary to the propagation of the gospel of the Kingdom. Also we observe in this declaration of independence from the Pharisaic custom of fasting another demonstration of the universalism incorporated by Jesus into his mission and message when he refused in the temptation experience to chain his gospel to the Temple and the Davidic monarchy, and when at Nazareth he indicated that his ministry would be parallel to the ministries of Elijah and Elisha to Gentiles. Again we see the reaffirmation of a previously revealed pattern in the emphasis in this reply to John's disciples on the note of joy as belonging to the gospel of the Kingdom. The gladness associated with a Jewish marriage week would be like that produced by the proclamation of the year of Jubilee. And so if there was to be joy with the announcement of the "acceptable year of the Lord," there would be similar joy among the "sons of the bridechamber" as they waited upon the bridegroom in the course of the marriage week.

In highly important points, therefore, this declaration of Jesus on fasting reveals his fidelity to the patterns of character and purpose he had accepted.

2. *While revealing himself as the Bridegroom, Jesus shows that he is also the Servant of Jehovah.* "Can the children of the bridechamber mourn, as long as the bridegroom is with them?" Jesus asked the disciples of John, and then continued with the highly significant statement,

"but the days will come, when the bridegroom will be taken from them, and then shall they fast." This statement has aroused much controversy among scholars. It is agreed by many that this is a reference by Jesus to his death, but a number of scholars maintain that the words could not have been uttered by Jesus at this early period in his ministry. This position is taken on the assumption that at this early date Jesus could not have foreseen his death. The reply to this view is that Jesus saw himself at the commencement of his ministry as the Servant of Jehovah and he had determined to be true to his character as the Servant. His knowledge of Isaiah's portrait taught him that the Servant was the *Suffering* Servant; the opposition of his own home people at Nazareth and the conflict he had just experienced with the Pharisees in Matthew's house (Mark 2:16f.; Matthew 9:11ff.; Luke 5:30ff.) were a portent for him of things to come; the consciousness of who he was and the sense of his divine mission, revealed in his conduct and words from the baptism on; his nearness to God and his knowledge of human nature and the world of evil—these factors were sufficient to make it possible for Jesus at this early period to foresee his death and make this prediction about the days when the Bridegroom would be "taken away" from the "sons of the bridechamber."

But there is a further objection made to the appearance of these words at this point. It is voiced by C. J. Cadoux in this manner: "If we consider these words (Mark 2:19; Matt. 9:15a; Luke 5:34) by themselves, apart from their immediate sequel . . . they depict the early ministry in Galilee as a joyous and triumphant episode—a picture not easily harmonized with the certainty of approaching tragedy. Nor can we suppose that it resembled marriage festivities for the Disciples only, while Jesus kept his sorrow hidden in his heart; for that would imply a strong lack of sense of reality on his part—either he (the Bridegroom) was himself rejoicing, or there could have been no rejoicing at all."[4] Dr. Cadoux's point is that it was impossible for Jesus to act the part of the Bridegroom and at the same

[4] ***The Historic Mission of Jesus,*** **Harper and Brothers, New York, p. 189 f. By permission.**

time be aware of his coming death. But does not this view reveal a rather poor understanding of what the mission of Jesus meant to Jesus himself? If Jesus foresaw that his death was inevitably linked with his *historic* mission; if he foresaw that as the Servant of Jehovah there was no escaping the divine imperative to be always in all circumstances the Servant of Jehovah, and if he accepted from the beginning even the possibility that in the conflict with evil the Servant must suffer and die, would the knowledge that he would die in the act of supreme loyalty to God cause him unhappiness? Rather would not the determination to die as an expression of devotion to his cause, faithfulness to his character, and obedience to the will of God, and the knowledge that he would die because of these things, give to him an inner sense of joy and peace that would enable him to be in truth the Bridegroom who himself was happy and shared his happiness with others? This is undoubtedly the explanation of this capacity of Jesus for both gladness and the knowledge of sorrowful days to come. And so we hold that the ability of Jesus to foresee his death and its implications is in harmony with the character he represents his to be in referring to himself as the Bridegroom. There is in fact a profound consistency in these two concepts—the concept of the Servant of Jehovah and the Bridegroom, as applied to Jesus, and there is perfect relevancy in their fusion in his person. If Dr. Cadoux misses the mark at this point in his apprehension of the mind of Jesus concerning his mission, he also falls short in his appreciation of the capacities of ordinary mortals. Many saints of God have awaited death with a joyousness and an inner peace that were infectious, and in their cases there was no conviction, as in the case of Jesus, that death for them would be the expression of a great divine purpose.

At this stage Jesus does not reveal to the disciples outright that he is to die. He says, "The days will come when the bridegroom *will be taken from them.*" In so far as the disciples are concerned his words are ambiguous; the statement is an enigma for the disciples; they are not yet prepared for the interpretation of the words as meaning the death of their Master; this will come later. For the present they can enjoy without interruption the joyous days of the marriage week. This admission that the disciples did not understand Jesus' words as a prophecy of his death does not diminish their importance as revealing the conviction of Jesus that he would die.

But what of the statement of Jesus that when the Bridegroom was taken away the "sons of the bridechamber," that is, the disciples, would fast? Is this, contrary to what has been derived from the teaching of Jesus at this point, an admission that his disciples may adopt the custom of fasting at his death and that it will be right for them to do so? Does he mean to say that when the day of his "taking away" comes the cloth of the Kingdom shall have been shrunk so that it may be attached appropriately to the old garment of Pharisaism, or that the unfermented wine that is the gospel of the Kingdom shall have reached that stage of fermentation, so that it may be poured into the old wineskins of formal religion? Jesus meant nothing of the sort. As an expression of genuine sorrow, fasting, whether it belong to Pharisaic religion or to some other, is always appropriate. It would certainly be appropriate as an expression of the sorrow of the disciples when he was taken from them. At the time the disciples of John came to Jesus with their question Jesus indicated the inappropriateness of fasting as an expression of sorrow—there was no sorrow for the disciples to express in this "marriage week" with the Bridegroom; he also indicated by the use of the parables that followed its inappropriateness at all times as a religious rite to be attached to the gospel of the Kingdom.

II. The Coming One

(Matthew 11:2-19; Luke 7:18-35)

Another question comes to Jesus, this one directly from John the Baptist. It is, "Art thou he that should come, or do we look for another?" As reported by both Matthew and Luke, the question is literally, "Are you the Coming One, or shall we go on expecting another?"

Again the ministry of John provides the backdrop against which it is possible to delineate the person and mission of Jesus. This much-debated question and the reply it brought forth are, as has been suggested, of immeasurable importance in the search for the mind of Jesus concerning himself. The question from John is one of those rare direct inquiries demanding an answer from Jesus that reveals his conviction concerning himself. The question is framed in such a way that identification of the personage referred to is possible—"Are you the Coming One?" Since we are able to identify the Coming One, we shall be able by studying the reply of Jesus to gain further light upon his conception of his person.

The exchange between Jesus and John is important also, as we have said, because Jesus gives a revelation concerning himself on the basis of things that have happened. It is significant that Jesus says to the disciples of the Baptist, "Go your way, and tell John what things ye have seen and heard." It will be interesting to discover whether or not this revelation that Jesus makes of his thinking concerning himself, coming after he has witnessed the effect of his words and works, is consistent with the convictions previously made known.

This incident, involving the question of John and the reply of Jesus, is admittedly difficult of interpretation, but it is not so difficult as to justify the prolonged failure of scholars to understand it. A more careful study of the language and the context would have eliminated errors of interpretation that have been perpetuated through the centuries. This also would have done something to remove the stigma that incorrect interpretations have fastened upon John the Baptist. This study, we trust, will make some contribution in that direction.

The record of this incident belongs to Q, the *Logia,* it being a part of the non-Markan material common to Matthew and Luke. It is therefore from one of the primary sources of the Gospels.

As we begin the study of this question and the reply of Jesus, it is important to understand clearly the form of the question. The question and the description of the manner of its sending come only after a very significant statement in Matthew. This statement is, "Now when John had heard in the prison the works of Christ, he sent two of his disciples." To render more faithfully the Greek text the statement of Matthew should read, "Now John hearing in the prison the works of *the Christ*," et cetera. The article occurs here with *Christ* and its presence is designed to convey the definiteness of the term. It is clearly the purpose of the Gospel writer to convey the truth that John accepted Jesus as *the Christ*. Luke writes, before giving the account of the sending of the disciples of John to Jesus: "And the disciples of John showed him of all these things." Luke had previously related the story of the healing of the centurion's servant, and the raising of the widow's son at Nain, so that these were the "things" concerning which the disciples of John informed their master. John accepted these as the works of *the Christ*. There was therefore no doubt in the mind of John that Jesus was *the Christ*. It was not the purpose of the Baptist to secure from Jesus the assurance that he was *the Christ*.

John's question was not inspired, as has been so often alleged, by lack of faith—lack of faith in Jesus as the Christ or lack of faith in God. John's question indicates the presence of a perplexity in his mind concerning the person and mission of Jesus, and his question is the expression of a sincere desire to resolve this perplexity. It was not, as has so often been alleged, the result of doubt that had been produced by the long and gruelling imprisonment in the fortress of Herod Antipas at Machaerus. The tribute paid by Jesus on this very occasion to his Herald should have guided the interpreters away from the error of ascribing to John a weakening of his faith. The portrait painted by Jesus is of a strong man, one who would be faithful in all circumstances and to the end. "What went ye out to see?" Jesus asked of the people as the disciples were making ready to return to John, "A reed shaken with the wind?" No! John was no reed that quivers with every passing breeze. "A man clothed in soft raiment?"—a fop without principle or stability who might shift his opinion on the slightest provocation? No! such men live in the palaces of kings, not in the desert among wild beasts! John was not such a person, he was a prophet and more than a prophet—he was the Herald of the Christ, the one of whom Malachi spoke when he said, "Behold, I send my messenger before thy face." Such was the character of the tribute paid by Jesus to his Herald. It is very clear that Jesus did not think that John's question indicated that the faith of the Baptist was wavering.

What, then, inspired John's question? As we have suggested, the question was the expression of a desire to resolve a perplexity that had arisen in the mind of John concerning the person and work of Jesus. The perplexity was born of disappointment on the part of John—disappointment that there was something missing from the ministry of Jesus, something John had hoped to see and had not seen. His disappointment was not rooted in any doubt that Jesus was *the Christ*—this is quite plain—but in the fact that there was a lack in the ministry of Jesus that he could not understand. This conviction of something missing in the ministry of Jesus was based upon John's conception of Jesus revealed in his public declarations concerning him, and reports of the nature of Jesus' work and teaching that had come to him. These reports indicated that Jesus was failing to conform to certain features of the portrait that John had painted. Why was Jesus not conforming to these features of the portrait? This was John's perplexity.

What were the features of John's portrait of Jesus that Jesus was apparently failing to fulfil? They are to be seen in the words of the Baptist reported by Matthew and Luke (Matthew 3:11-12 and Luke 3:16-17). Matthew's version follows:

> I indeed baptize you with water unto repentance: but he that cometh after me is mightier than I, whose shoes I am not worthy to bear; he shall baptize you with the Holy Ghost, and with fire: whose fan is in his hand, and he will throughly purge his floor, and gather his wheat into the garner; but he will burn up the chaff with unquenchable fire.

Let us study closely the characteristics of this personage described by John. He is described as "he that cometh after me." The entire sentence in the Greek is *ho de opisō mou erchomenos ischuroteros mou estin,* "He that cometh after me is mightier than I." Particular attention should be given to the words *ho . . . erchomenos,* "he that cometh." They are strongly suggestive of the language used by John in the question addressed to Jesus, "Are you the Coming One (*ho erchomenos*), or shall we go on looking for another?" It can be seen, of course, that in the sentence, "He that cometh after me is mightier than I" the Greek article is removed by several words from the participle it modifies, "*erchomenos,*" so that we are not justified in translating, as in the question addressed by John to Jesus, "the Coming One," but it is quite proper to translate literally "The after-me Coming One is mightier than I," in which case the personage described is the Coming One whose advent is after John's.

On the basis of John's language in describing the great personage of whom he was the Herald, we are warranted in concluding that he thought of him as a definite personage known as the Coming One. In any event it is profitable to examine further the characteristics of the person spoken of by John. He is a person whose chief endowment is *power*. He is to baptize with the Holy Spirit and with fire. He comes equipped with a winnowing fan so that he can speedily separate the wheat from the chaff. The wheat he will store in his garner but the chaff he will consign to unquenchable fire. The symbolism is plainly intended to convey the truth that the great person to come is a mighty judge capable of distinguishing good from evil and commissioned with authority to reward the righteous and execute judgment upon the unrighteous. With this portrayal agree the other words of John foretelling the dispensation of which he was the Herald and suggesting the character of the work to be done by the great person of this dispensation: "And now also the axe is laid unto the root of the trees: therefore every tree which bringeth not forth good fruit is hewn down, and cast into the fire" (Matthew 3: 10). Here again is the display of power, the speedy separation of good and evil, the sudden execution of judgment against the wicked.

This, then, is John's conception of the great Person who

is to usher in the Kingdom of Heaven. If this Messiah of John's thinking is not the Messiah of popular expectation, he bears resemblance to the Mighty Person, who according to tradition would restore the Davidic kingdom, destroy the enemies of Jehovah and set up the reign of righteousness upon the earth. We may grant that the Messiah of John's hopes is less materialistic and more spiritual than the Messiah of traditional Jewish expectation, but he shares with the popular concept the characteristic of power, power to destroy the enemies of Jehovah, execute judgment, reward the righteous and establish without delay the righteous reign of Jehovah upon the earth. The Kingdom of Heaven in John's view is apocalyptic in nature and the Messiah of his hopes is an apocalyptic figure.

The reports that came to John of Jesus' work disturbed him because they afforded no evidence that Jesus was acting like the person described by John in those deliverances on the banks of the Jordan. These works of healing, and even the raising of the dead were appropriate to the ministry of the Christ, John reasoned, but what of the display of power, the execution of judgment against the enemies of Jehovah, the separation of the righteous from the unrighteous, the establishing in power of the Kingdom of righteousness? Jesus was the Christ—very well; but might there be another, one yet to come who would perform the mighty deeds John promised would be done by the great person of whom he spoke when he preached by the Jordan?

This great personage whose image haunted John's mind was not unknown to the prophets. It is probable that he was known and discussed in a limited way among the rabbis and pious folk of Jesus' day. He was the *Coming One.* It is difficult, to be sure, to make out his image in prophecy but dim outlines may be traced.

There is the suggestion of such a person in Daniel 9:26, a verse from a passage which has occasioned much controversy. The meaning of this passage (9:24-27) will always be obscure, but it must be considered in our search for light upon the problem under discussion. In the Authorized Version verse 26 reads:

And after threescore and two weeks shall Messiah be cut off, but not for himself: and the people of the prince that shall come shall destroy the city and the sanctuary; and the end thereof shall be with a flood, and unto the end of the war desolations are determined.

According to Montgomery the events described in the passage (9:24-27) from which the verse is taken took place in the Maccabean age.[5] R. H. Charles in his commentary on Daniel likewise sees these events as transpiring in the Maccabean age.[6] Our interest here is not in the actual historical fulfilment of Daniel's prophecy, but in the speculation aroused by the prophecy among the people of Jesus' day. There is evidence that this passage was the source of apocalyptic speculation in the time of Jesus, and this is the matter of importance for the present discussion. Jesus himself referred to this passage when in his great eschatological discourse he instructed the disciples concerning their conduct at the *fall of Jerusalem* by saying, "When ye therefore shall see the abomination of desolation, spoken of by Daniel the prophet, stand in the holy place (whoso readeth, let him understand:)," et cetera (Matthew 24:15). The "abomination of desolation" referred to is spoken of in Daniel 9:27, the concluding verse of the passage of which our verse 26 is an integral part. Charles translates the phrase "A horror that appalleth" and makes it a reference to "the altar and image of Zeus."[7] Jesus evidently referred it to the image or standard of Caesar which he knew would be set up someday in the not-too-distant future in the holy place of the Temple.

Josephus, the Jewish historian, found in Daniel prediction of the destruction of the Jewish state by the Romans. He likely had in mind the prophecy under discussion in saying, "In the very same manner Daniel also wrote concerning the Roman government, and that our country should be made desolate by them."[8] Paul's reference in 2 Thessalonians 2:4f. to the "man of sin" who "as God sitteth in

[5] Daniel in the *International Critical Commentary*, p. 386.

[6] *A Critical and Exegetical Commentary on The Book of Daniel*, The Clarendon Press, Oxford, p. 244-250.

[7] *Op. cit., ad loc.*, p. 251 f.

[8] *Antiquities of the Jews*, X, xi, 7, Whiston's Translation, John C. Winston Company, Philadelphia. By permission.

the temple of God'' and who must be ''revealed'' before the ''day of Christ'' is very probably a reflection of the influence of Daniel 9:27 and its prophecy concerning the ''abomination of desolation.''

Thus the evidence is strong that Daniel 9:24-27 was the subject of apocalyptic interest and speculation in the first century. The point of interest as a consequence of this is that in Daniel 9:26 mention is made of both Messiah and ''the prince that shall come.'' These are separate personalities. In the Hebrew version ''Messiah'' is *mashiaḥ*—''an anointed one,'' rendered in the Septuagint as *Chrisma.* ''The prince that shall come'' in the Hebrew text is *nagidh habba,* rendered by the Septuagint as *tō hēgoumenō tō erchomenō.*

It is not our purpose to attempt the interpretation of this verse. Our purpose is to show that it belongs to a passage that had apocalyptic significance in the first century and that its terminology would be strongly suggestive to first century minds of a distinction in the persons of the Christ and The Coming One. The ''Messiah'' in this verse is *mashiah,* which in Hebrew is ''anointed one.'' This is the term that came to be accepted as applying to the coming Christ. The ''prince'' referred to is described as *habba,* ''the Coming One.'' As shown above the Septuagint renders this by the Greek *ho erchomenos* (in the Instrumental case). The character of ''the prince that shall come'' is worth noting. It is prophesied that ''the people'' of this prince ''shall destroy the city and the sanctuary; and the end thereof shall be with a flood, and to the end of the war desolations are determined.'' This statement might easily be taken by apocalyptically minded people of the first century as referring to the work of judgment and retribution to be performed by the Coming One in establishing his kingdom in power. It is entirely possible that John the Baptist had come under the influence of such apocalyptic thinking. Whether he was influenced by this prophecy in Daniel it is not possible to say with certainty. What we do know is that when he made his famous inquiry of Jesus he made a clear distinction between ''the Christ'' and ''the Coming One,'' and we know further that in his messages by the Jordan the Kingdom he preached was strongly apocalyptic in character and the great person he spoke of as coming after him was an apocalyptic figure.

A comment by Edersheim is appropriate at this point. He says: "The designation 'The Coming One' (*habba*), though a most truthful expression of Jewish expectancy, was not one ordinarily used of the Messiah. But it was invariably used in reference to the Messianic age, as the *Athid labho,* or coming future (literally, the prepared for to come), and the *Olam habba,* the coming world or Aeon. But then it implied the setting right of all things by the Messiah, the assumption and vindication of his power. In the mouth of John it might therefore mean chiefly this: Art Thou He that is to establish the Messianic Kingdom in its outward power, or have we to wait for another?"[9]

There is this additional evidence that the representation we have made of John's thinking is correct. John conceived of himself as incarnating the spirit of Elijah and thus fulfilling the prophecy in Malachi 4:5: "Behold, I will send you Elijah the prophet before the coming of the great and dreadful day of the Lord." This is seen in the style of his dress, which was similar to Elijah's (Mark 1:6; Matthew 3:4; 2 Kings 1:8). He also copied Elijah's mode of life and manner of preaching. Jesus spoke of John as "Elijah" (Mark 9:12f.; Matthew 17:11-13). (The Fourth Gospel represents John as denying that he was Elijah, but this need only mean that he denied that he was the actual reincarnation of the prophet. (See John 1:21.) As "Elijah," his duty, according to Malachi, was to prepare the people for "the coming of the great and dreadful day of the Lord." This was the "day of Jehovah," the day when the enemies of Jehovah would be put to flight and the righteous reign of Jehovah would be established in power. As the Herald of the Coming One fulfilling this prophecy in Malachi, John would also think of himself as the "messenger" of Malachi 3:1 who would prepare the way of the Lord. He was designated as this "messenger" by Jesus (Matthew 11:10; Luke 7:27) and by Mark (1:2).

---

[9] *Op. cit.,* p. 668.

The description Malachi gave of the One whose way the messenger would prepare certainly influenced the thinking of John and helped inspire the apocalyptic coloring of his concepts of the Messiah and the Kingdom. The description follows: "The Lord, whom ye seek, shall suddenly come to his temple, even the messenger of the covenant, whom ye delight in: behold, he shall come (Hebrew *ba,* Septuagint *erchetai*), saith the Lord of hosts. But who may abide the day of his coming? and who shall stand when he appeareth? for he is like a refiner's fire, and like fullers' sope." (3:1f.). This person, if not called outright *habba,* the Coming One, is described as "coming" (Hebrew *ba*). His character is in keeping with what has been suggested from other sources as characteristic of the Coming One.

III. The Reply of Jesus

We come now to the reply of Jesus to John's question. According to Matthew it was: "Go tell John the things which you hear and see: The blind are receiving their sight, the lame are walking, the lepers are being cleansed and the deaf are hearing, and the dead are being raised up and the poor are having the good tidings preached to them. And blessed is that one, whoever he is, who shall not be caused to stumble in me."

The words of Jesus echo two passages from Isaiah, 35:5-6 and 61:1, the latter being a part of the passage used by Jesus in his declaration in the synagogue at Nazareth. From it Jesus selects for the reply to John the words, "the poor are having the good tidings preached to them." Isaiah 35:5-6 reads:

> Then the eyes of the blind shall be opened, and the ears of the deaf shall be unstopped. Then shall a lame man leap as an hart, and the tongue of the dumb sing: for in the wilderness shall waters break out, and streams in the desert.

It will be seen that the two passages from Isaiah account for Jesus' references to the blind, the deaf, the lame, and the poor, but not for the references to the cleansing of the lepers and the raising of the dead. There is obvious similarity of this description of the gracious blessings of Jesus' ministry to that quotation in the synagogue at Nazareth forecasting the character of his ministry. Both in this reply to John and in the Nazareth declaration the outcasts, the sufferers, and the underprivileged are the beneficiaries of Jesus' activity. In both statements the poor are described as having the glad tidings preached to them and the blind as receiving sight. It is evident from the reply to John that Jesus plainly conceives of himself at this point in his ministry as the same Servant of Jehovah he conceived himself to be when he made his appearance in the synagogue at Nazareth. The choice of another passage of Scripture making possible the inclusion of the lame and the deaf as beneficiaries of his ministry, and the addition without help of scriptural background of the lepers and the dead as beneficiaries, is indicative of Jesus' joyous conviction that God had abundantly vindicated the choices which he had made. He had witnessed the power of God at work through the Servant in a manner exceeding his hopes. His faith in the patterns he accepted in the wilderness had been abundantly justified! God was blessing and vindicating the Servant of Jehovah!

And so by this reply to John Jesus said in effect: "What I am is sufficient; the works I am performing as the Christ bear testimony to the presence and power of God with me; it is not necessary that I be other than I am."

Jesus clearly refused to accept the designation of himself as the Coming One of John's thinking. Just as clearly he re-affirmed his conviction that he was the Servant of Jehovah. If there was in his own mind the conviction that he was the Coming One, his reply leaves no doubt that he would accept the prophesies referring to the Coming One only in a spiritualized sense. He would have none of the materialistic portrayal of the Coming One as applying to himself. Nor would he allow the apocalyptic characterization of the Coming One to be applied to himself. He would indeed be the Judge who would separate the righteous from the unrighteous; he would be Malachi's "messenger of the covenant" who would be "like a refiner's fire, and like a fuller's sope," but he would fulfil his office as Judge, not as a mighty apocalyptic figure by a sudden establishment of the Kingdom in power, but as the Servant of Jehovah and the Christ who preached glad tidings to the poor, cleansed the lepers, opened the eyes of the blind and the ears of the deaf, healed the lame and raised the dead.

Jesus thus renounced apocalypticism as belonging to the nature of the Kingdom of Heaven! This is the highly significant and revolutionary truth that comes to light in the reply of Jesus to John. It must not be taken as a denial of the clear teachings of Jesus concerning the *eschatological*[10] aspects of the Kingdom. Jesus did have a doctrine of *last things.* This doctrine is clearly seen in his teachings concerning the consummation of the Kingdom and the *Parousia* or Coming of the Son of Man. But contrary to the view of Albert Schweitzer and other scholars who have been influenced by his theory, Jesus did not conceive of the Kingdom as coming suddenly in power during his lifetime or at his death. It was this apocalyptic conception of the Kingdom that Jesus renounced in his reply to John. This is the explanation of the statement by Jesus that follows, made to the crowds after he had given his answer to the question of the Baptist:

> Among them that are born of women there hath not risen a greater than John the Baptist: notwithstanding he that is least in the kingdom of heaven is greater than he. And from the days of John the Baptist until now the kingdom of heaven suffereth violence, and the violent take it by force. For all the prophets and the law prophesied until John (Matthew 11:11-13).

What do these much misunderstood words of Jesus mean? In the first place, they do not mean, as has been suggested, that John was not in the Kingdom. Jesus says, "He that is least in the kingdom of heaven is greater than he." His meaning was that the person who because of his childlike disposition had become in truth a "little one" of the Kingdom, understanding and accepting its spiritual

---

[10] John Wick Bowman has performed a valuable service in his book, *The Intention of Jesus*, The Westminster Press, Philadelphia, in distinguishing between apocalypticism and eschatology. According to Bowman, Jesus was an anti-apocalyptist. See his book, p. 52.

nature was greater than John, who, though a prophet, misunderstood the true nature of the Kingdom, and was therefore not "great" in the Kingdom, but in fact smaller than the "little ones."

It is now possible from the study we have made of John's concept of the Kingdom to understand why Jesus said, "From the days of John the Baptist until now the kingdom of heaven suffereth violence, and the violent take it by force." John was an apocalyptist, preaching a Kingdom that would come in suddenly with power. That was why the Kingdom suffered violence and violent men took it by force from the days of John! John's preaching had conveyed wrong ideas concerning the Kingdom; men had taken those ideas and had done violence to the Kingdom. John had fed the fires of apocalyptic dreams, and now he was pondering the question of whether or not his dream of a kingdom to come with power would not be fulfilled in the Coming One, one who would do what Jesus was not doing: "throughly purge his floor . . . gather his wheat into the garner . . . burn up the chaff with unquenchable fire." This was why he that was "least" in the Kingdom was greater than John—this, and the fact that the "least" one in the Kingdom accepted as sufficient the work of Jesus the Christ and felt no need for the Coming One to bring in the Kingdom with power.

In his reply to John Jesus reaffirms his adherence to a *spiritual* Kingdom of God and reveals his calm assurance in himself as the Servant of Jehovah. We may hope with confidence that the good and brave man in the fortress of Machaerus understood the import of his Master's words and died in the peaceful conviction that he performed his duty according to the light that had been granted to him.

IV

CAESAREA PHILIPPI

1. *The Son of Man and His Cross*

Mark 8:27-9:1; Matthew 16:13-28; Luke 9:18-27

The narrative of the withdrawal of Jesus with the twelve to the regions of Caesarea Philippi is abundant in its supply of data bearing upon the messianic consciousness of Jesus. There is related here the first effort of Jesus to bring the twelve to an admission of the view which he himself held concerning his person. The incident embraces the first attempt of Jesus to prepare the twelve for the shock of his impending death. From this point on everything in the ministry points toward the final journey to Jerusalem and focuses around the fact of Jesus' death. The reaction of Jesus to the confession of Peter, "Thou art the Christ, the Son of the living God," provides evidence of the utmost value in the search for the actual pattern of his thinking about himself. There is the added fact of importance that he refers to himself in this context as the Son of Man, which introduces a new factor in our search for the mind of Jesus.

Pressing questions therefore arise in connection with the consideration of this epochal conversation at Caesarea Philippi. Did Jesus accept the designation of himself by Peter as "the Christ, the Son of the living God"? If so, what does this acceptance reveal as to his thinking—who to him was "the Christ, the Son of the living God"? What was the meaning of the subsequent statement of Jesus concerning the "rock" upon which he would build his church? What is the significance of the revelation of his coming death that he makes immediately following the great confession of Peter? What is revealed in the use by Jesus in this context of the self-designation, "Son of Man"? Does he by the announcement of his impending death and by his use of this self-designation betray a departure from previously accepted patterns? Or is he true to these patterns? Is there significance to be attached to the announcement of his death as he refers to himself as the "Son of Man"? These and other questions press for answers as we approach the study of this epochal conversation.

The plan of approach to the study will be first to analyze the reply of Jesus to the confession of Peter with a view to determining what the reply reveals as to the thinking of Jesus concerning himself; second, a careful investigation of the use by Jesus here and in other contexts, of the title "Son of Man"; third, a study of the statement of Jesus concerning his impending death and its significance in this context.

At the outset a word should be said concerning the sources of the narrative of the withdrawal to Caesarea Philippi. Matthew and Luke follow Mark in their narratives, so the primary source is Mark. However, Matthew makes an addition in the verses 16:17-19, the passage having to do with the "rock" upon which the church was to be built, a narrative which is peculiar to his Gospel. It belongs, therefore, to the source used by Matthew alone, designated as *M*. It should be recalled also that the withdrawal to the regions of Caesarea Philippi occurred not more than nine months and possibly not more than six months before the crucifixion. If the ministry of Jesus lasted two and a half years, this withdrawal took place about eighteen months after the reply of Jesus to the question of John the Baptist; if the ministry was three and a half years in length, then the withdrawal took place two and a half years approximately after the question came from John.

We come now to the analysis of the passage.

I. Preparation for the Confession

The manner in which Jesus prepared the minds of Peter and the other disciples for the all-important question concerning their conviction about him should not escape us.

According to Matthew, Jesus introduced the conversation with the inquiry: "Who do men say that I the Son of Man am?" Mark and Luke do not record Jesus' designation of himself as the Son of Man in this initial question. Luke has the question: "Who say the multitudes that I am?"

Jesus did not ask this question for information. He must have been informed, even better than the twelve, concerning the tides of current opinion. He was familiar with the sentiments of the multitudes concerning himself. His purpose in asking the question was to create the basis for a contrast between the right and the wrong conceptions of himself. He wished to bring the disciples to see a delineation of his true character against the background of the inadequate and incomplete conceptions the multitudes held concerning him. One of these inadequate conceptions was the popular notion that Jesus was John the Baptist risen from the dead. This idea gained circulation as a result of the superstitious dread of Herod Antipas who when he heard of the works of Jesus expressed the opinion that Jesus was the man he had beheaded come to life (Mark 6:14; Matthew 14:1f.). Thus it will be seen that *superstition and fear* had produced one of the popular and superficial conceptions of the person of Jesus. Another popular idea reported by the disciples was that Jesus was Elijah or Jeremiah or one of the prophets. This notion was evidently based upon the popular belief that one of the prophets—most likely Elijah (see Malachi 4:5)—or a prophet "like unto Moses" (Deuteronomy 18:18), would appear before the coming of the Messiah. A willingness to do honor to Jesus by placing him in the line of the prophets, coupled with an unwillingness to accept the revolutionary demands of his gospel, may be described as the basis of this popular and inadequate conception of Jesus. It may be classified as produced by *rationalization.*

Having thus drawn the attention of the twelve to the current popular notions concerning himself, Jesus now addresses them with the very pointed personal question, "But who say ye that I am?" In the Greek the question is opened with the personal pronoun and upon it the emphasis of voice is to be placed, so that the question is, "But who say *ye* that I am?" The presence of the adversative conjunction *de* (but) and the emphatic position of the personal pronoun *humeis* (ye) indicate the purpose of Jesus to draw from the twelve a confession that will place their conviction about him in contrast with the superficial popular notions with which they were familiar. This careful preparation by Jesus of the minds of the twelve for the great confession that follows enhances the value of his reaction to Peter's reply as a clue to his own thinking. It indicates his search in the minds of the disciples for a conception above and beyond the popular ideas upon which they had reported. It indicates that he was leading them on to a higher conception that he himself held. Did the reply of Peter reveal a conviction in the minds of the disciples that would match that held by Jesus himself? Will the reaction of Jesus to Peter's confession reveal Jesus' own mind concerning himself? We shall see.

II. The Confession of Peter and the Response of Jesus

Matthew represents Peter as saying in the reply to Jesus' question, "Thou are the Christ, the Son of the living God." Mark records that he replied, "Thou art the Christ," while Luke states that he said, "The Christ of God." All agree that Peter confessed Jesus as *the Christ*. There is no cause to doubt that Matthew's fuller answer represents substantially what Peter said in Aramaic, the language in which Jesus and the twelve commonly spoke. This fuller reply will be used as the basis of the discussion of the meaning of Peter's words in their relation to the thinking of Jesus.

Before examining the meaning of Peter's reply some attention will be given to the response of Jesus that is given by Matthew. In this response it is evident, first of all, that *Jesus accepts Peter's designation* of him as "the Christ, the Son of the living God." This is shown by Jesus' words, "Blessed [happy] art thou, Simon Barjona: for flesh and blood hath not revealed it unto thee, but my Father which is in heaven." That which by being expressed makes Peter "blessed" in the eyes of Jesus, and is expressed according to Jesus as a result of a divine revelation, is beyond question accepted as true by Jesus. Again it must be observed that *Jesus sees Peter's confession as produced by divine revelation*. This is the meaning of his words, "flesh and blood hath not revealed it unto thee, but my Father which is in heaven." With this statement Jesus indicates the manner in which the knowledge that he was the Christ the Son of the living God came to himself, for we are not to suppose that the manner in which the knowledge came to Peter was superior to that by which Jesus received it. Jesus thus reveals that knowledge of the truth concerning himself is divinely given and does not come by rationalization. Flesh and blood, neither Peter's flesh and blood, nor that of the multitudes who were his contemporaries and who could think of Jesus only as John the Baptist or one of the prophets, was capable of producing the exalted confession that Jesus was the Christ, the Son of the living God. It was Peter's faith and his faith only that enabled the Spirit of God to bring him to this exalted conception of Jesus. The recognition of this fact by Jesus is evidence of his appreciation of the difficulty involved in the acceptance by others of the exalted opinion that he himself held concerning his person. Perhaps here is one clue to the care with which he had guarded the secret of his Messiahship from the public. This matter of accepting his Messiahship involved far more than the saying of words—it involved a spiritual condition in confessors that made them receptive to a revelation from God. That spiritual condition was a condition directly antithetic to "flesh and blood"; it could therefore be produced only by a revolutionary change in the natural state of man. God reveals the great secret that Jesus is the Christ the Son of the living God only to those who are spiritually prepared for the revelation. This is an awe-inspiring revelation, a mighty truth of cosmic and eternal significance; it must be reserved for those who are capable of receiving it!

The vast importance of this great confession is further emphasized by the words of Jesus that follow in Matthew's narrative. As a result of his confession of Jesus as the

Christ, the Son of the living God, Peter is "confessed" by Jesus, even as he confessed Jesus.[1] The "confession" that Jesus makes of Peter is made possible because he has confessed Jesus as the Christ, the Son of the living God. It is a confession, the substance and import of which might be made to any individual who makes the confession that Peter made in the manner in which he made it. Indeed, the conversation that brought forth Peter's confession was begun, not with Peter individually but with all the twelve. It is proper, therefore, to consider the confession of Peter as expressive of the sentiment of the twelve as a whole, Judas excluded, and the response of Jesus as applicable in principle to all the disciples with the exception of the traitor, who never arrived at that condition of spiritual receptivity that would enable him to receive a divine revelation that Jesus was the Christ, the Son of the living God. Jesus' "confession" of Peter was, "Thou art Peter." This was simply the name Jesus had given Peter when he chose him to be one of the twelve. (Mark 3:16; Luke 6:14). Its significance lay in the fact that its meaning was "a stone." The Aramaic word was *kēphas,* if we are to judge by the Greek transliteration given in John 1:42. The Greek word was *petros.* Jesus' words then amount to the confession that Peter has become by his confession what his name implies—a stone. In effect Jesus says, "You are Peter indeed." Jesus now makes a play upon words which has occasioned endless controversy, and it is not our purpose to give undue space to a consideration of the matter. It seems quite clear, however, that Jesus intended to convey a distinction in this use of the word *petros* and the use of *petra* in the statement, "and upon this rock (*petra*) I will build my church." If no distinction was intended in the terms, it seems impossible to rely upon language to convey meanings. It would have been very natural for the author of the narrative to have written *petrō,* the locative form of *petros,* instead of *petra* here, if no distinction in the terms was intended. The fact that the term *petra* survived

[1] The form of Jesus' statement, "And I say *also* unto thee," *(kagò de soi legō)* indicates that he on his part is now making a confession in response to Peter's.

the many copyings that preserved it in the ancient manuscripts and made it a part of the critical text serves as an argument for the tenacity of the form, different only by the final letter from *petros*, and ought to suggest its distinctiveness. But the argument is made that Jesus spoke in Aramaic and that Aramaic is not capable of making the distinction between a *stone* and *rock*. It is hazardous to make any such claim in respect to the inability of Aramaic to express this or that, because of the lack of Aramaic literature upon which to base an opinion. There are Aramaic passages and a number of Aramaic words here and there in the Old Testament, but outside of these there is not a single literary work in existence composed in the Aramaic language that existed in written form in the first century. Our knowledge of Aramaic terms is therefore considerably limited. Brown, Driver, and Briggs[2] give as the Aramaic word for "stone," *eben*, and show the similarity of the Aramaic word for "cleft" or "fissure" to the root of the Hebrew word, *sela*, "crag," "cliff," [3] translated in many places "rock." This would suggest the capacity of the Aramaic to differentiate between a stone and a large ledge rock. We shall accept the record of our Greek-speaking reporter, therefore, as preserving the distinction in the terms which Jesus made when he uttered the original statement. The statement of Jesus then becomes: "You are *Petros*, and upon this *rock* I will build my church."

Now if we are faithful to the usual meaning of *petros*, we know that Jesus was not thinking of Peter as the foundation upon which the church was to be built, for, while *petros* may be a large or a small stone, it would not refer to a stone sufficiently large to serve as the foundation of a building. But *petra* is precisely the term that would be applied to a foundation stone because it means a large ledge rock. Jesus does mean, however, that *Peter belongs to the foundation of the church, is a part of that foundation.* The play upon words suggests that Peter is a *petros*, a stone, from or like the *petra*, the ledge rock which is to be

[2] *Hebrew and English Lexicon of the Old Testament* under *eben*, p. 6.
[3] *Op. cit.*, p. 700.

the foundation of the church. Peter is a part of the foundation, but he is by no means all of it. There are other stones hewn from this ledge rock. By this figure, then, Jesus declares that he will build his church upon a foundation composed of individuals, Peter and others like him, who confess Jesus as the Christ, the Son of the living God as a result of a revelation from God. This is the most reasonable interpretation of these difficult words. By it the foundation of the church is neither Peter as the first "bishop" of the church, nor Peter's faith, but a group of living men who by faith accepted Jesus as the Christ, the Son of the living God. The facts of history bear out the prophecy of Jesus. The men who by faith accepted the revelation of his Messiahship and Sonship and confessed the revelation to the world as their own conviction did indeed constitute the foundation of the church.

This memorable statement reflects the exalted conception that Jesus held concerning himself. The "church" to which he refers as *my* church is the new assembly which he sets over in contrast with the old assembly of Israel. The old assembly (*ḳahal*) was constituted at Mt. Sinai when the people of Israel were called to the mount to hear the words of Jehovah. This is referred to as "the day of the assembly" in Deuteronomy 9:10. In the Septuagint both here and in Deuteronomy 4:10 this day is the *hēmera ekklēsia*. This was the day when the covenant was given and the people became the *ḳahal*, the assembly, the *ekklēsia* of the Septuagint. The foundation upon which this assembly was constituted was the law, symbolized in the two tables of stone brought by Moses from the Mount. The primacy of *faith* is seen in the constitution of the new assembly, and in this it is in sharp contrast with the old assembly of Israel. The foundation of the new assembly is made of men of faith—men who because of their faith receive the revelation from God that Jesus is the Christ, the Son of the living God, and confess him as such. Who is Jesus in his own eyes? That he sees himself as establishing a new assembly in contrast with the old assembly of Israel, a new assembly to take the place of the old, is quite evident from the content of his statement and the language in which it is couched. That he thinks of himself as the founder of this new assembly is indicative of his assent to Peter's ascription to him of the exalted title: the Christ, the Son of the living God.

The primacy of faith in the thinking of Jesus is re-emphasized in his declaration concerning the building of his church. Men of faith are to form the foundation of his *ekklēsia.* This declaration reflects the great affirmation of the primacy of faith in the wilderness and the reaffirmation of its primacy in the synagogue at Nazareth. The indestructibility of this new *ekklēsia* is promised by Jesus. His promise is that "the gates of Hades shall not prevail against it," by which is meant that death shall not overcome the church. That which is built upon men of faith cannot be destroyed by death.

Jesus further emphasizes the exalted opinion that he entertains concerning himself by his promise to give to Peter the keys of the Kingdom of Heaven. In this change of figures Peter becomes a steward who is charged with the responsibility of keeping a house. He carries the keys, not actually of a house but of a realm: the Kingdom of Heaven. By his great confession he has become a steward of the Kingdom with the authority of opening the doors of the Kingdom that those who wish to enter may come in. Likewise Jesus commissions him with the authority of "binding" and "loosing"; that is, of forbidding and permitting. "Whatsoever thou shalt bind on earth," Jesus promises, "*shall have been bound* [the construction is the Future Perfect Passive and not the simple Future Passive] in heaven: and whatsoever thou shalt loose on earth *shall have been loosed in heaven.*" This promise to Peter of authority to "bind" and "loose" is a promise of Heaven's inspiration and guidance for declaring the way of God to men. Whatever Peter forbids shall be that which Heaven has forbid; whatever Peter permits shall be that which Heaven has allowed. These words of Jesus are directed to Peter because it was he who as spokesman of the twelve made the great confession that Jesus was the Christ, the Son of the living God. There is no reason to believe that

Jesus excluded from this promise of authority others who would meet the conditions of stewardship met by Peter.

Again, Jesus reveals a conviction that he sustains a genuinely unique relationship with God. He sees himself vested not only with power to constitute a new assembly, but also with authority to confer upon his disciples the right to open the doors of the Kingdom of Heaven to men and to promise these disciples that they will have Heaven's guidance in declaring to men the way of God. Who but one who conceived himself to be the Son of God and the Messiah of Israel could make such promises?

III. The Meaning of the Title "The Christ, the Son of God"

The term *mashiah*, "anointed one," was likely the term used by Peter in his confession of Jesus as "the Christ." It is not found in the Old Testament as specifically referring to the Messiah, as we have seen, unless its use in Daniel 9:25f. is a reference to the Messiah. The term was frequently applied to the king or a priest, as "the anointed" of Jehovah. It was most likely commonly understood in the first century as referring to the Messiah. The woman of Samaria is reported by John as saying to Jesus, "I know that Messias cometh, which is called Christ" (4:25). "Messias" here an effort of the Greek to transliterate *mashiah*, while "Christ" in the Greek is *Christos*. The term is found in the parables of Enoch (written, according to Charles, between 94 and 79 B.C.) as referring to the Messiah (48-10 and 52:4).[4] In the *The Odes and Psalms of Solomon* (middle of the first century B.C.) the Greek *Christos* (17:36), referring to the messianic king, is in all probability a translation of the Hebrew *mashiah*.)[5]

Of more significance than the terminology, however, is the combination in two important Old Testament passages of the messianic king and Son of God ideas. The first of these passages is 2 Samuel 7:12-16, in which Jehovah is

[4] The section of the parables in which these references are found was originally written in Hebrew, according to Charles. See his *The Book of Enoch*, pp. lxi-lxix. The Mss. used by Charles was in Ethiopic.

[5] The original of this work was also Hebrew. See *The Odes and Psalms of Solomon*, by J. Rendel Harris, p. 38.

represented as instructing the prophet Nathan what he is to say to David. The passage follows:

> And when thy days be fulfilled, and thou shalt sleep with thy fathers, I will set up thy seed after thee, which shall proceed out of thy bowels, and I will establish his kingdom. He shall build an house for my name, and I will establish the throne of his kingdom for ever. I will be his father, and he shall be my son. If he commit iniquity, I will chasten him with the rod of men, and with the stripes of the children of men: but my mercy shall not depart away from him, as I took it from Saul, whom I put away before thee. And thine house and thy kingdom shall be established for ever before thee: thy throne shall be established for ever.

The person of whom it is said here "I will be his father, and he shall be my son" was, of course, Solomon. The failure of Solomon to combine in himself this ideal concept of king and son of Jehovah was well known. It was also a well-known fact that the throne of David failed. This promise therefore that David's throne would be "established for ever" had been left unfulfilled. Thus the prophecy of the ideal Messiah-King remained an ideal that had never been realized. In view of his acceptance of the designation of himself as Son of God, it is altogether likely that Jesus saw in himself the realization of the ideal Messiah-King portrayed in this prophecy. The point of importance in this prophecy is that the ideal king pictured here is thought of as Jehovah's son—*"I will be his father, and he shall be my son"* are the words of Jehovah concerning the coming king. We see here perhaps the germ of the idea that the Messiah was to be in a peculiar sense Jehovah's Son. We should not lose sight of the fact that the throne of this ideal Messiah-King-Son was to be "established for ever." The suggestion is not that this prophecy was necessary to Jesus' consciousness that he was the Son of God, but that it aided him in locating himself and his mission in the great prophetic patterns of Israel. The location of himself in these prophetic patterns would not only confirm his faith in himself and his mission, it would also enable him to give direction to his ministry. Another value to this identification of himself with the great patterns of prophecy would be the demonstration for posterity of the fact that in Jesus the purposes of God in history were fulfilled.

In the eighty-ninth Psalm we find again the combination of the Messiah-King-Son concepts. Significant verses in this psalm are "I have made a covenant with my chosen, I have sworn unto David my servant, Thy seed will I establish for ever, and build up thy throne to all generations (3-4). . . . I have found David my servant; with my holy oil have I anointed him (20): . . . He shall cry unto me, Thou art my father, my God, and the rock of my salvation. Also I will make him by firstborn, higher than the kings of the earth" (26-27).

When Jesus accepted Peter's identification of himself as the Christ, the Son of the living God, he may well have conceived of himself as the realization of the ideal Messiah-Son of these passages. In any event there is abundant evidence in the Synoptics that he conceived of himself as sustaining an absolutely unique relationship to the Father. He taught his disciples to say "our" Father, but he commonly spoke of God as *my* Father. Every recorded instance of his use of the expression "my Father" reveals in Jesus the consciousness of a normal (for him) but unique intimacy with God. (See Matthew 7:21; 10:32f.; 12:50; 15:13; 16:17; 18:10, 19, 35; 20:23; 24:36; 25:34; 26:29, 39, 53; Luke 2:49; 22:29.) There is also the extraordinary passage, Johannine in its tone, preserved only by Matthew and coming presumably from his special source *M*. It is: "I thank thee, O Father, Lord of heaven and earth, because thou hast hid these things from the wise and prudent, and hast revealed them unto babes. Even so, Father: for so it seemed good in thy sight. All things are delivered unto me of my Father: and no man knoweth the Son, but the Father; neither knoweth any man the Father, save the Son, and he to whomsoever the Son will reveal him" (11:25-27). The passage speaks for itself concerning the consciousness of Jesus that he was in a unique sense, a sense in which other men were not, the Son of God.

There remains in this connection the testimony of Jesus before the high priest. According to both Matthew and

Mark (Mark is likely the primary source), Jesus admitted at his examination before the Sanhedrin that he was the Son of God. (Mark 14:61-64; Matthew 26:63-66). It is clear that the Sanhedrin understood this to be the testimony of Jesus because it immediately pronounced him guilty of blasphemy and condemned him to death. According to Mark's account the question of the high priest was, "Art thou the Christ, the Son of the Blessed?" "Son of the Blessed" could mean, of course, only "Son of God." To this question Mark represents Jesus as saying, "I am." The question, according to Matthew, was put after the high priest had put Jesus on oath with the words, "I adjure thee by the living God." The demand was then made, "that thou tell us whether thou be the Christ, the Son of God." Matthew records the reply of Jesus as, "Thou hast said." This was tantamount to Jesus' saying, "You said in the words, 'the Christ, the Son of God' what is true about me." The manner in which this confession is obtained speaks for its inherent truthfulness as a revelation of the mind of Jesus. It was with reluctance that he gave the testimony; his conduct indicates that he would never have volunteered the claim that he was the Son of God, and that it was made only because the high priest by his question made a reply inescapable. This reluctance to make public display of his conviction that he was the Son of God is evidence that the conviction was very sacred to him. The consciousness of his unique relationship to God was not to be a plaything of cynical and unappreciative men; nor yet was it to be the cause for boasting or display. It was first of all his own possession, the mighty bulwark of his mission and ministry. Again, it was the great secret to be shared with those who like Peter were men of faith who would gladly say, "Thou art the Christ, the Son of the living God." To others it was to be revealed only because to refuse to reveal it would be disloyalty to himself and to truth.

The fact that the Sanhedrin pronounced Jesus guilty of blasphemy and condemned him to death on the basis of his admission that he was the Son of God is proof that the claim was considered in the popular mind as extraordinary and dangerous. The Sanhedrin understood fully the implication of Jesus' confession: it indicated he conceived of himself as more than an ordinary man, as sustaining a unique relationship to God.

IV. The Use of the Title "Son of Man" by Jesus

We pass on to a consideration of the use by Jesus of the title, Son of Man. We meet with the title in important connections in the present context. It was Jesus' chosen self-designation. He consistently referred to himself by this title. The title in the Synoptics is never used by others in referring to Jesus (except in Luke 24:7). Without consideration of its use in John's Gospel and not counting duplications where the Synoptics combine in relating the same incident, we find forty-six references by Jesus to himself as the Son of Man. A study of the mind of Jesus concerning himself demands therefore a careful investigation of his use of the title. If by diligent inquiry the meaning of the title to Jesus can be determined a flood of light will be thrown upon the conviction which Jesus held concerning himself and his mission. We shall likewise be able to tell whether by use of this self-designation Jesus reveals that in his character which is consistent with his decisions in the wilderness, his declaration at Nazareth, and his reply to John the Baptist.

According to Matthew's narrative the conversation of Jesus with the disciples at Caesarea Philippi is opened with the question, "Who do men say that I the Son of man am?" In the account of the revelation of his impending death that follows, Matthew omits reference to the Son of Man, but the title is contained in the statement of Jesus as given by Mark and Luke. Mark says, "And he began to teach them, that the Son of man must suffer many things," et cetera. All three Gospels represent Jesus as referring to himself as the Son of Man when at the conclusion of this conversation he refers to the "coming" of the Son of Man "in glory," while Matthew adds one more reference in the final statement, "Verily I say unto you, There be some standing here, which shall not taste of death, till they see the Son of man coming in his kingdom."

The uses of the term in this context are sufficiently challenging, but it will be necessary to survey the entire field of Jesus' use of the title in order both to understand its use here and its meaning as an index to the conviction that Jesus held concerning himself.

A survey of the occurrence of the title in the Synoptics shows that there are five classifications into which the uses fall. These are seen in the following divisions.

1. *The eschatological use.* Matthew 13:41—"The Son of man shall send forth his angels." 16:27—"The Son of man shall come in the glory of his Father with his angels." 24:27—"So shall also the coming of the Son of man be." 24:37—"So shall also the coming of the Son of man be." 24:39—"So shall also the coming of the Son of man be." 24:44—"In such an hour as ye think not the Son of man cometh." 25:31—"When the Son of man shall come in his glory." Mark 8:38 (Luke 9:26)—"of him also shall the Son of man be ashamed." Luke 12:8—"him shall the Son of man also confess before the angels of God." 12:40—"The Son of man cometh at an hour when ye think not." 17:22—"Ye shall desire to see one of the days of the Son of man." 17:24—"So shall also the Son of man be in his day." 17:30—"Thus shall it be in the day when the Son of man is revealed." 18:8—"When the Son of man cometh, shall he find faith on the earth?" 21:36—"and to stand before the Son of man." There are fifteen uses in this category.

2. *Use in reference to the Resurrection.* Matthew 17:9—"Tell the vision to no man, until the Son of man be risen again from the dead." Mark 9:9 (Matthew 16:28)—"He charged them that they should tell no man . . . till the Son of man were risen from the dead." There are four instances in which the title is used with reference both to Jesus' sufferings and his resurrection. (See Mark 8:31; Luke 9:22; Mark 9:31; 10:33f.; Luke 24:7).

3. *Its use in relation to the sufferings and death of Jesus.* Matthew 12:40—"So shall the Son of man be three days and three nights in the heart of the earth." Matthew 26:2—"The Son of man is betrayed to be crucified." Matthew 8:20 (Luke 9:58)—"The Son of man hath not where

to lay his head." Mark 9:12 (Matthew 17:12)—"It is written of the Son of man, that he must suffer many things." Mark 9:31 (Matthew 17:22; Luke 9:44)—"The Son of man is delivered into the hands of men, and they shall kill him." Mark 10:33 (Matthew 20:18; Luke 18:31)—"The Son of man shall be delivered unto the chief priests, and unto the scribes; and they shall condemn him to death." Mark 10:45 (Matthew 20:28)—"The Son of man came not to be ministered unto, but to minister, and to give his life a ransom for many." Mark 14:21 (Matthew 26:24)—"The Son of man indeed goeth, as it is written of him." Mark 14:21 (Matthew 26:24; Luke 22:22)—"Woe to that man by whom the Son of man is betrayed!" Mark 14:41 (Matthew 26:45)—"Behold, the Son of man is betrayed into the hands of sinners." Mark 8:31 (Luke 9:22)—"the Son of man must suffer many things." Luke 22:48—"Betrayest thou the Son of man with a kiss?" Luke 24:7—"The Son of man must be delivered into the hands of sinful men, and be crucified, and the third day rise again." There are thirteen instances of the use of this title in this category.

As noted, four of the uses of the title apply also to the resurrection of Jesus. They are in Mark 8:31 (Luke 9:22); Mark 9:31; 10:33f.; and Luke 24:7. The latter is the only recorded instance in the Gospels where the title is used by any other than Jesus (except in John 12:34), and here it is in a quotation of his words by the two men in shining garments at the tomb. This is also the only recorded use of the title in the Gospels after the narrative of the death of Jesus. There are only three other uses of the title beyond this point in the New Testament: in Acts 7:56, where Stephen says. "I see the heavens opened, and the Son of man standing on the right hand of God," and in Revelation 1:13 and 14:14.

4. *Its use in relation to the earthly ministry of Jesus.* Matthew 12:32—"Whosoever speaketh a word against the Son of man, it shall be forgiven him." Matthew 13:37—"He that soweth the good seed is the Son of man." "Matthew 16:13—"Who do men say that I the Son of man am?" Matthew 11:19 (Luke 7:34)—"The Son of man came eat-

ing and drinking." Mark 2:10 (Matthew 9:6; Luke 5:24)—"The Son of man hath power on earth to forgive sins." Mark 2:28 (Matthew 12:8; Luke 6:5)—"the Son of man is Lord also of the sabbath." Luke 11:30—"As Jonah was a sign unto the Ninevites, so shall also the Son of man be to this generation." Luke 12:10—"Whosoever shall speak a word against the Son of man, it shall be forgiven him." (This is in a different context from that of Matthew 12:32). Luke 19:10—"For the Son of man is come to seek and to save that which was lost." The number of uses in this category is nine.

5. *Its use in connection with the extension of the Kingdom in power.* Matthew 10:23—"Ye shall not have gone over the cities of Israel, till the Son of man be come." 16:28—"There be some standing here, which shall not taste of death, till they see the Son of man coming in his kingdom." 24:30—"And then shall appear the sign of the Son of man in heaven." Mark 13:26 (Matthew 24:30; Luke 21:27)—"And then shall they see the Son of man coming in the clouds." Mark 14:62 (Matthew 26:64)—"Ye shall see the Son of man sitting on the right hand of power, and coming in the clouds of heaven." 17:26—"So shall it be also in the days of the Son of man." 22:69—"Hereafter shall the Son of man sit on the right hand of the power of God."

There are seven uses of the title classified under this heading. Casual reading of the references here will at once raise questions. The reader will recognize similarities between most of these sayings and those classified under the heading, "The eschatological use." The reasons for interpreting these uses of the title as non-eschatological will appear in the discussions that follow, especially under the topics, "Was Jesus the Apocalyptic Son of Man?" "The Son of Man in the 'Little Apocalypse,' " and "The Day of the Son of Man in Luke 17:20-37."

A scrutiny of the uses of the title listed above enables us to reach a preliminary conclusion of importance, namely, *the title is always one of dignity.* It has often been claimed that the title was used by Jesus to emphasize his humanity.

A careful study of the uses of the title will not bear out this view. Even when Jesus uses the title in speaking of his sufferings and death, there is the unmistakable implication of the exalted position of the one who is to suffer and die. The same is true of the use of the title with respect to Jesus in his earthly ministry and work. In this category, which should be most revealing of the emphasis of the title upon the humanity of Jesus, if such emphasis were intended, we find that "the Son of man hath power on earth to forgive sins"; "the Son of man is lord also of the sabbath"; "the Son of man came to seek and to save that which was lost," et cetera. If "the Son of man came eating and drinking," he stands over in exalted contrast with John the Baptist; if one may be forgiven for speaking a word against the Son of Man, the promise of forgiveness is bracketed with a warning that he who speaks against the Holy Spirit will not be forgiven, the implication being that the Son of Man is worthy to be considered in this connection with the Holy Spirit.

Unquestionably Jesus conceived of this self-designation as one of dignity, as one that suggested his exalted position and character. When we come to a consideration of the historical background of the title we shall find that its use by Jesus as a title of dignity is very much in keeping with its pre-New Testament usage.

V. The Historical Background

It is quite important for the understanding of Jesus' use of the title to know something of its historical usage before he laid hold of it as the characteristic designation of himself. Jesus did not manufacture the title or take it out of thin air. Indeed it was its historical usage that made it available for his purpose. Let us see therefore what that usage was.

The expression "son of man" was adopted by the prophet Ezekiel as a designation of himself. It occurs in the book of Ezekiel over eighty-five times as the title by which the prophet is addressed. In Hebrew the term is *ben adham.* This is rendered by *whios anthrōpou* in the

Septuagint. The article occurs in neither the Hebrew nor the Greek. In Ezekiel it is little more than a form of address and has little significance in so far as the prophet's message or mission is concerned. It probably does express the prophet's humility and his desire to be identified closely with the people to whom he ministers. It is improbable that Ezekiel's use of the term has any connection with its use by Jesus.

It is different, however, with the one, but all-important appearance of the term in Daniel. This occurrence is at Daniel 7:13-14. The passage follows:

> I saw in the night visions, and, behold, one like the Son of man came with the clouds of heaven, and came to the Ancient of days, and they brought him near before him. And there was given him dominion, and glory, and a kingdom, that all people, nations, and languages, should serve him: his dominion is an everlasting dominion, which shall not pass away, and his kingdom that which shall not be destroyed.

"One like the Son of man" here is in the Hebrew *kevar enash,* "one like *a* son of man," which in the Septuagint is rendered without the article *hōs whios anthrōpou.* While the article is absent here the term applies very definitely to the exalted supernatural personage described. Charles interprets the expression here as referring not to an individual but to "the faithful remnant of Israel." [6] This view is not beyond question, but even if the reference were to the nation and not to an individual, the point that concerns us is the interpretation that would be given to the term by readers of later generations. Charles comes to our aid here. He believes that the use of the title in the parables of Enoch was derived from this passage in Daniel and comments: "but a whole world of thought lies between the suggestive words in Daniel and the definite rounded conception as it appears in Enoch. In Daniel the phrase seems merely symbolical of Israel, but in Enoch it denotes a supernatural person. In the former, moreover, the title is indefinite, 'like a son of man,' but in Enoch it is per-

---

[6] *A Critical and Exegetical Commentary on The Book of Daniel,* The Clarendon Press, Oxford, p. 187.

fectly definite and distinctive, 'the Son of Man' "[7] We may be certain that if the author of Enoch took Daniel's "Son of man" to be an individual, the people of the first century A.D. thought of the prophecy as referring to an individual. To the mind of Jesus and to those familiar with this passage in Daniel the title "Son of Man" would be suggestive of this exalted individual who "came with the clouds of heaven," whose "dominion is an everlasting dominion, which shall not pass away."

The words of Jesus in the so-called "Little Apocalypse" (Mark 13:1-37) where the Son of Man is described as "coming in the clouds with great power and glory," and his reference in his defense before the Sanhedrin to the Son of Man's "coming in the clouds of heaven" (Mark 14:62) are echoes of this passage in Daniel. The fact that he refers in the "Little Apocalypse" (marginal reading) to "the abomination of desolation, spoken of by Daniel the prophet," (Mark 13:14), substantiates the view that he echoes here Daniel's words concerning the Son of Man.

We pass on now to the consideration of certain passages in the parables of Enoch, passages that undoubtedly had some influence in the choice by Jesus of the title "Son of Man" as his self-designation. A suggestion that the book of Enoch (from which the parables are taken) was read in the first century and had some influence on early Christian thinking is seen in the fact that the book was used by Jude. (See Jude, v. 14.)

The first of the passages from Enoch relevant to our study is 46:1-6. It is, according to the translation of Charles[8] from the Ethiopic:

And I saw one who had a head of days, And His head was white like wool, And with Him was another being whose countenance had the appearance of a man, And his face was full of graciousness, like one of the holy angels. And I asked the angel who went with me and showed me all the hidden things, concerning that Son of Man, who he was, and whence he was, (and) why he went with the Head of Days? And he answered and said unto me: This is the Son of Man who hath righteousness, With whom dwelleth righteousness,

[7] *The Book of Enoch*, or *I Enoch*, Translated from the Editor's Ethiopic Text, by R. H. Charles, The Clarendon Press, Oxford, Second Edition, p. 307.
[8] *Op. cit.*, p. 85 f. Used by permission of the publishers.

And who revealeth all the treasures of that which is hidden, Because the Lord of Spirits hath chosen him, And whose lot hath the preeminence before the Lord of Spirits in uprightness for ever. And this Son of Man whom thou hast seen Shall raise up the kings and mighty from their seats, [And the strong from their thrones] And shall loosen the reins of the strong, And break the teeth of the sinners; [And he shall put down the kings from their thrones and kingdoms] Because they do not extol and praise Him, Nor humbly acknowledge whence the kingdom was bestowed upon them. And he shall put down the countenance of the strong, And shall fill them with shame. And darkness shall be their dwelling, and worms shall be their bed, And they shall have no hope of rising from their beds, Because they do not extol the name of the Lord of Spirits.

In his comment on the occurrence of the title "Son of Man" in this passage, Charles states that the Greek phrase which the Ethiopic translator had before him was undoubtedly *ho whios tou anthrōpou,* the full title with the definite article before "son" and again before "man." The title always occurs in this form in the Gospels. In his discussion of the character of the Son of Man in the parables, in connection with the analysis of this passage, Charles calls him the Messiah and says: "The Messiah is conceived in the parables as (1) the Judge of the world, (2) the Revealer of all things, (3) the Messianic Champion and Ruler of the righteous." In the Appendix to his work he says: "The Son of Man as portrayed in the parables is a supernatural being and not a mere man. He is not even conceived as being of human descent, as the Messiah in *I Enoch* 90:37. He sits on God's throne, 51:3, which is likewise His own throne, 62:3, 5, 69: 27, 29, possesses universal dominion, 62:6, and all judgment is committed unto him, 41:9, 69:27. . . . This title, with its supernatural attributes of superhuman glory, of universal dominion and supreme judicial powers, was adopted by our Lord." Charles then proceeds to show how the title underwent transformation in Jesus' use of it, but of this more later.[9]

In the parables are other suggestive passages. At 69:27 we read: "And he sat on the throne of his glory, And the sum of judgment was given unto the Son of Man," and at 69:29: "For that Son of Man has appeared, And has seated

[9] *Op. cit.,* p. 307.

himself on the throne of his glory, And all evil shall pass away before his face, And the word of that Son of Man shall go forth, And be strong before the Lord of Spirits."[10] The allusion here to the Son of Man's sitting "on the throne of his glory" seems to be reflected in the words of Jesus before the Sanhedrin: "Ye shall see the Son of man sitting on the right hand of power." There is not this form of allusion in Daniel 7:13-14 to the assumption by the Son of Man of kingly authority, though Daniel speaks of the "dominion, and glory, and a kingdom" that are given to him. There is greater similarity in the words of Jesus to the statement in Enoch than to the words of Daniel.

There is further evidence that Enoch's picture of the Son of Man was known to Jesus. In the parables at 62:1f. it is said, "And thus the Lord commanded the kings and the mighty and the exalted, and those who dwell on the earth, and said: 'Open your eyes and lift up your horns if ye are able to recognize the Elect One.' And the Lord of Spirits seated him on the throne of His glory." The parable continues (5-6), "And one portion of them shall look on the other, And they shall be terrified, And they shall be downcast of countenance, And pain shall seize them, When they see that Son of Man sitting on the throne of his glory. And the kings and the mighty and all who possess the earth shall bless and glorify and extol him who rules over all, who was hidden."[11] Jesus stood before the high priest, the supreme religious official of the nation, and the Sanhedrin, the supreme court of Israel, when after testifying that he was the Christ, he declared "and ye shall see the Son of man sitting on the right hand of power, and coming in the clouds of heaven" (Mark 14:62). It was as if Jesus was thinking of the high priest and the members of the Sanhedrin as among "the mighty and exalted" in the passage in Enoch who would be "terrified" and "downcast of countenance" when in time they would see "that Son of Man, sitting on the throne of his glory."

Enoch further relates of the Son of Man: "from the be-

---

[10] From *The Book of Enoch*, p. 140 f.
[11] *Op. cit.*, p. 122, ff.

ginning the Son of Man was hidden, And the Most High preserved him in the presence of His might, And revealed him to the elect" (62:7).[12] As a possible reflection of the influence on the mind of Jesus of this idea of the "hidden" state of the Son of Man, coupled with his "revealing" to the "elect," was the charge of Jesus to the disciples "that they should tell no man that he was the Christ" (Matthew 16:20), and his admonition after the transfiguration "that they should tell no man what things they had seen, till the Son of man were risen from the dead" (Mark 9:9).

Much prominence is given in the parables of Enoch to angels and their activity. There is no mention of angels in Daniel 7:13-14. There are statements of Jesus with reference to the work of the Son of Man which seem to reflect this emphasis upon angels in Enoch. At Mark 13:26f. Jesus is quoted as saying: "And they shall see the Son of man coming in the clouds with great power and glory. And then shall he send his angels, and shall gather together his elect from the four winds, from the uttermost part of the earth to the uttermost part of heaven." In the parable of the tares (Matthew 13:36-43) the "reapers" are angels who are sent out by the Son of Man at the end of the age to "gather out of his kingdom all things that offend."

Before leaving this study of suggestive passages in Enoch, attention should again be directed to the fact that the Son of Man of the parables is also the "Anointed" of the Lord. He is described thus at 48:10 and 52:4. Charles takes the term as synonymous with "Messiah."[13] This being so, the Ethiopic term in the text used by Charles was a translation of the Greek *Christos.* It is clear that the office of Messiah is combined with that of the Son of Man in Enoch. It is also quite clear that in the thinking of Jesus the two were combined. At Caesarea Philippi he referred to himself as the Son of Man and accepted Peter's designation of himself as "the Christ, the Son of the living God."

---

[12] *The Book of Enoch, op. cit.,* p. 124.
[13] *Op. cit.,* p. 95.

VI. Why Did Jesus Adopt the Title Son of Man?

With this sketch of the historical background of the term before us, there yet remains the question as to why Jesus adopted it as the designation of himself. Is it possible to reconcile the exalted, supernatural, unearthly figure of the Son of Man in Daniel and the parables of Enoch with the portrait the Synoptics give us of Jesus? The only satisfactory answer to this question is that the Son of Man concept in Daniel and Enoch was transformed in the mind of Jesus. We shall make it our aim to discover in what way the concept was transformed in its use by Jesus, for only thus shall we be able to determine what the title revealed as to his conviction about himself.

Before investigating this transformation that the Son of Man concept underwent in the mind of Jesus it is possible to give several practical reasons for Jesus' use of the title: (1) It seems probable that the title was not a popular designation of the Messiah. Perhaps the question of the Jews recorded in John's Gospel (12:34) is indicative of the ignorance of the people generally as to the implications of the title. Here John says: "The *people* answered him, We have heard out of the law that Christ abideth forever: and how sayest thou, The Son of man must be lifted up? who is this Son of man?" The Synoptics represent Jesus as guarding very carefully from the public the fact of his Messiahship. It hardly would have been in keeping with this representation for Jesus to have adopted a title by which he frequently referred to himself that suggested at once to the populace that he was the Messiah. (2) The very enigmatic nature of the title would challenge curiosity. It would thus serve like a parable to stimulate the interest of the spiritually alert while providing for Jesus a shield from the superficial and unspiritual. There were many of Jesus' listeners who could if they would grasp the implications of his use of the title. The book of Enoch was popular among the Pharisees and the book of Daniel was available to all. Those who were genuinely interested in the message of Jesus would be enabled to see in his use of the title intimations of his Messiahship and dignity. (3) Jesus employed the title with the deliberate intent of placing on record for the sake of posterity his estimate of himself. It is strange that in the attempt to estimate the person of Jesus men have so often overlooked the aid they might have received from the name that he chose for himself and what it reveals of his consciousness of his person and mission. This name is so inextricably interwoven with the Gospel record and the life and work of Jesus that it cannot possibly be eradicated by criticism of any imaginable sort. Acceptance of the Gospel records demands acceptance of the fact that Jesus used the title Son of Man to refer to himself. Its use is a part of the record of his life and work. Any estimate of the person of Jesus must take its use into consideration—if for no other reason than that it is an index of what he thought of himself. To many what he thought of himself is exceedingly important in determining what he actually was. (4) The title provided Jesus with a mode of expression that would enable him to demonstrate the synthesis of two great and apparently opposing concepts of the Messiah. These were the concept of the Son of Man and the concept of the Suffering Servant. The title Son of Man served the purpose of preserving the dignity and glory of a Messiah who would be rejected and crucified upon a Roman cross. At the same time the fusing of the Suffering Servant concept with that of the Son of Man served to purge the old messianic ideal of its materialistic and crude apocalyptic features. In a number of passages the future glory of the Son of Man and his sufferings are brought into close juxtaposition and relationship, as is true of the narrative of the withdrawal to Caesarea Philippi, where the revelation of Jesus' impending death immediately follows the great confession of Peter. It is this remarkable fusion of the Suffering Servant concept with that of the Son of Man that will occupy our attention in the chapter that follows. It is necessary, however, before taking up this aspect of our study to face a problem that the present discussion poses. We have said that the fusing by Jesus of the Suffering Servant concept with that of the Son of Man served to purge the old messianic ideal of its materialistic and crude apocalyptic features. But this view would not be acceptable to many scholars who hold that Jesus was an apocalyptist in his thinking. These scholars would maintain that the very use of the term Son of Man by Jesus indicated his apocalyptic leanings. It is true that the title originated in apocalyptic literature, but it does not necessarily follow that by its use Jesus adopted the apocalyptic mode of thinking. We know that he spiritualized the prophecies relating to the restoration of the Davidic monarchy; we have seen that he refused to be a literalist in the interpretation of messianic prophecies. There is no reason to believe that he would be more literalistic in his interpretation of the description of the Son of Man in the parables of Enoch. However the problem is not so easily disposed of as these valid generalizations suggest. It is necessary to study in some detail the question as to whether or not by his use of the term Son of Man Jesus indicated his expectation of the sudden and powerful establishment of the Kingdom of God upon the earth—either during his ministry or very soon after his death. There are statements strongly suggestive of this expectation on the part of Jesus.

VII. Was Jesus the Apocalyptic Son of Man?

The question is an acute one and occupies a large place in New Testament criticism. Albert Schweitzer, following older scholars who before him had struck out in the direction of the position which he adopted, makes the "eschatological" theory the key to an understanding of Jesus' ministry. His view has had considerable influence upon New Testament scholarship. By "eschatological" Schweitzer, in fact, means "apocalyptic," as we shall see. The terms are quite closely related, but they do not mean the same thing and there has been confusion in their use. "Eschatological" has to do with the theory and doctrine of last things. "Apocalyptic" is a system or method of indicating through visions and symbols God's immediate intervention in the natural order by supernatural means. There was always an eschatology in the literature of Israel, and eschatological hope is prominent in the writings of the prophets. The apocalyptic literature and the apocalyptic ideal were characteristic of the religious thinking of the first two centuries before Christ and in some measure of the New Testament period. It was the latter period that produced the greatest apocalypse of all, the book of Revelation.

And now to come to Schweitzer's theory. According to Schweitzer the mind of Jesus was dominated from beginning to end by the "eschatological" idea. He expected, Schweitzer claims, the sudden coming in of the Kingdom of God first when he sent out the twelve on their initial mission described in Matthew 10. Proof that Jesus expected the end of the age with his *Parousia* at this time is found in Matthew 10:23. When the Kingdom failed to come in Jesus decided that the pre-messianic tribulation which was to have come upon all must now fall upon himself alone. "In the secret of his passion which Jesus reveals to the disciples at Caesarea Philippi the pre-messianic tribulation is for others set aside, abolished, concentrated upon himself alone, and that in the form that they are fulfilled in his own passion and death at Jerusalem. That was the new conviction that had dawned upon him. He must suffer for others . . . that the Kingdom might come." According to Schweitzer Jesus went to Jerusalem to precipitate the *Parousia* and the coming in of the Kingdom by giving himself in death that "the debt which weighed upon the world" might be discharged. It was his confident expectation that immediately upon his death the *Parousia* would take place and the Kingdom would come in.[14] Of course he erred a second time. In Schweitzer's view Jesus conceived of the Son of Man as the supernatural being who would be revealed with the *Parousia* and the coming in of the Kingdom.[15]

Our first reply to the view of Schweitzer will be to point out his misunderstanding of the language of Matthew 10:23, the crucial passage of his whole theory, and his failure to give due regard to the context of this verse. The statement in 10:23, upon which Schweitzer's theory rests, in the Authorized Version reads: "Ye shall not have gone over the cities of Israel, till the Son of man be come." The words are addressed by Jesus to the twelve as he sends

[14] *The Quest of the Historical Jesus*, p. 386-395.
[15] *Op. cit.*, p. 357, 360.

them out upon their first mission. According to Schweitzer, "He tells them in plain words that he does not expect to see them back in the present age. The Parousia of the Son of man, which is logically and temporally identical with the dawn of the Kingdom, will take place before they shall have completed a hasty journey through the cities to announce it."[16] Schweitzer's eye was on evidence for his theory, and the context and the meaning of the Greek terms escaped him. Jesus' reference in this section to severe persecutions that were ahead of the disciples, including scourging in synagogues (v. 17), trials before governors and kings (v. 18), and the delivering up of brother by brother to death (v. 21), is clear evidence that the section beginning with verse 16 and continuing through the end of the chapter is not appropriate to this first mission of the twelve. On their first mission in Galilee it was unthinkable that the disciples would be scourged in synagogues, or that they would be brought before governors and kings or that any one of them would be delivered up to death by his brother. Such forms of persecution were to be encountered at later periods, and this section (Matthew 10:16-42) contains instructions for the conduct of the disciples in the periods that were to come after Jesus' death and after the fall of Jerusalem. Instructions for the twelve in the immediate situation and for the first mission are contained in Matthew 10:5-15. But not only does Schweitzer disregard his context here, he falls in with mistranslations of the Greek verbs in the statement in 10:23: "Ye shall not have gone over the cities of Israel, till the Son of man be come." Both verbs here are translated as if they were Perfects. "Ye shall not have gone over" is a Future Perfect idea, and "be come" is a Perfect in idea. The translation gives the impression that Jesus tells the twelve he will have "come" in some fashion before they complete their journey through the cities. The verbs, however, are not Perfects in Greek but Aorists, and what Jesus says in reality is "Ye shall not complete [*telesēte,* i.e., finish] the cities of Israel until the Son of Man *comes* [or *come*]."

---

[16] *Op. cit.,* p. 357.

The preceding statement will aid in the understanding of this one. Jesus has just said, "But when they persecute you in this city, flee ye into another." It will be seen, therefore, that this is a practical warning for the disciples in their future missions, against the loss of unnecessary time and effort. If the continuation of their work in one city is made impossible by persecution, they are to go on to another city where their message will not fall on deaf ears; they cannot finish the task of evangelizing the cities of Israel until the Son of Man comes. By this reference to the *coming* of the Son of Man Jesus refers to his "coming" at the fall of Jerusalem which will be discussed presently. It is quite plain that he does not expect the *Parousia* to take place before this journey of the twelve is completed. This is the crucial passage for Schweitzer in the development of his "eschatological" theory. If it can be thus demonstrated that it does not mean what he says it means, what becomes of his theory?

It is necessary to give attention now to the statement of Jesus made following the revelation of his death at Caesarea Philippi and pertaining to the "coming" of the Son of Man or the "coming" of the Kingdom with power during the lifetime of some of those who were his listeners. The Markan source, which is the primary source here, gives the statement thus: "Verily I say unto you, That there be some of them that stand here, which shall not taste of death, till they have seen the kingdom of God come with power." (Mark 9:1). Matthew's version of the statement is, "There be some standing here, which shall not taste of death, till they see the Son of man coming in his kingdom" (16:28). Luke says simply, "There be some standing here, which shall not taste of death, till they see the kingdom of God" (9:27).

Of course if by these words Jesus meant that immediately after his death the Kingdom of God was to come in *power* and the Son of Man would come in "the glory of his Father with the holy angels," we shall be compelled to admit that he was a thoroughgoing apocalyptist and that he fell in with the apocalyptic representation of the Son of Man in Daniel and in Enoch. Schweitzer fits these statements of

Jesus into his theory that when the Kingdom failed to come in with power with the sending out of the twelve he turned his face toward Jerusalem with the expectation that his death there would precipitate the coming in of the Kingdom and the revealing of the supernatural Son of Man. We submit that no such interpretation is necessary. In the first place, it should be observed that Jesus predicted that there were "some" ("certain ones" in the Greek) of those who stood in his presence who would not "taste of death" (i.e. die) until they saw the Kingdom or the Son of Man come in power. This form of the prediction might allow yet forty or fifty years for the fulfilling of the prophecy, since the members of the twelve were all young men. The statement cannot be pressed therefore as a prophecy of the *immediate* coming in of the Kingdom in power nor of the supernatural revelation of the Son of Man. The "coming" Jesus refers to here is not the *Parousia,* the eschatological "coming" of the Son of Man.

And yet Jesus does refer to his *Parousia,* his eschatological coming, in this same context. His reference is to the eschatological "coming" in the statement of Mark: "Whosoever therefore shall be ashamed of me and of my words in this adulterous and sinful generation; of him also shall the Son of man be ashamed, when he cometh in the glory of his Father with the holy angels" (8:38). Also Jesus refers to his *Parousia,* the eschatological "coming," when he is quoted by Matthew as saying: "For the Son of man shall come in the glory of his Father with his angels; and then shall he reward every man according to his works" (16:27). Now immediately following these statements in both Matthew and Mark are the references already discussed concerning those who would not taste of death until they saw the Son of Man coming in his Kingdom, or the coming of the Kingdom of God with power. The objection will doubtless be raised that Jesus could not have been speaking of two "comings" in the same conversation, but we ask, why not? A casual perusal of the uses of the title Son of Man by Jesus shows that he used it in connection with both his earthly ministry and the future work of the Son of Man. Is it necessary to think of the future work of the Son of Man as confined only to the eschatological "coming"? What of the extension and progress of the Kingdom after the conclusion of the earthly ministry of Jesus? Would it not be natural for him to think of this extension and progress of the Kingdom as the work of the Son of Man? And might he not think of the destruction of Jerusalem and the Temple, and the extension of the Kingdom incident to this event, as a "coming" of the Son of Man, or a "coming" of the Kingdom in power? We submit that this is a logical inference from his teaching. In order to establish this view a study will be made presently of the so-called "Little Apocalypse." In this study we shall see that Jesus makes a distinction between the "coming" of the Son of Man incident to the fall of Jerusalem, and his *Parousia,* or eschatological coming. Because of this distinction it is possible to interpret the "coming" of the Son of Man in Matthew 16:28, which according to Jesus some would see before they "tasted" of death, as an inauguration of the coming of the Kingdom in power incident to the destruction of the Jewish theocratic state. Jesus visualized this epochal event as setting the gospel of the Kingdom free from the strictures of Judaism and making possible a great forward movement for his gospel with universal conquest as its aim. This he saw as a "coming" of the Son of Man, or the "coming" of the Kingdom of God in "power." Jesus employed the imagery of apocalyptic to forecast this event, as we shall see. We shall also see that he by no means identified the *Parousia* with this event. The failure of interpreters to see that Jesus does preserve a distinction between the predictions concerning the fall of Jerusalem and his references to the *Parousia* has proved a hindrance to an understanding of Jesus' eschatological teaching. It has likewise led interpreters to picture Jesus as an apocalyptist, which is contrary to the real picture which the Gospels give of him. Jesus was not an apocalyptist, despite the fact that he employed apocalyptic imagery and the apocalyptic title "Son of Man" as his self-designation. He did have an eschatology, a doctrine of last things, however. His eschatology focused around the *Parousia* and the *Resurrection.*

If we accept the view that Jesus prophesied a "coming" of the Son of Man incident to the destruction of Jerusalem, we shall be able the better to understand his words when at his trial he said to the high priest, "Ye shall see the Son of man sitting on the right hand of power, and coming in the clouds of heaven" (Mark 14:62). Some of the men who condemned him to death doubtless lived to see the destruction of Jerusalem and the "coming" of the Son of Man in "power" as the Kingdom progressed in "power" after this event. Also the statements of Jesus respecting the appearing of the "sign of the Son of man in heaven" (Matthew 24:30), and the "coming" of the Son of Man "in the clouds" (Mark 13:26) become understandable, as will be shown in the discussion of the Son of Man in the "Little Apocalypse," if this view is accepted.

The truth of the matter is, therefore, that when Jesus speaks of the "coming" of the Son of Man it is necessary to interpret the reference in the light of the context and the logic of the passage containing the reference. We cannot be dogmatic always in designating one reference as "eschatological" and another as "non-eschatological." Perhaps Jesus designed that there would be a certain amount of mystery connected with his prophecies concerning the "coming" of the Son of Man. Doubtless he viewed the approaching fall of Jerusalem as a sort of type of his eschatological coming, and it is possible that this accounts in part for the interweaving of the prophecies relating to the fall of Jerusalem with those concerning the *Parousia*. If the prophecies are thus interwoven in the "Little Apocalypse," might there not have been in other passages references in the same context to the Son of Man's "coming" in power incident to the fall of Jerusalem and his *Parousia* at the end of time? Because of the probability that this is true, we repeat that Jesus was speaking of his eschatological coming in Matthew 16:27 when he said, "For the Son of man shall come in the glory of his Father with his angels; and then he shall reward every man according to his works," despite the fact that he says in the verse immediately following, "Verily I say unto you, There be some standing here, which shall not taste of death, till they see the Son of man coming in his kingdom.'' Our justification for classifying the first reference as eschatological, in addition to what has been said, is in the promise of Jesus that when the Son of Man comes he ''shall reward every man according to his works.'' It is difficult to refer the promise of such reward to a ''coming'' of the Son of Man incident to the fall of Jerusalem. The ''reward'' spoken of by Jesus is best understood as the final reward for all the faithful incident to the consummation of history in the *Parousia* of the Son of Man. Likewise it seems most natural and most in keeping with the logic of the words to attribute the warning of Jesus in Mark 8:38 to the eschatological coming of the Son of Man. ''Whosoever therefore shall be ashamed of me and of my words in this adulterous and sinful generation; of him also shall the Son of man be ashamed, when he cometh in the glory of his Father with the holy angels'' is a warning that is suggestive of the final judgment rather than of a prior ''coming'' of the Son of Man. It is strained to conceive of the Son of Man as being ''ashamed'' of unfaithful followers except in connection with his work as judge when all men appear before him for recognition or nonrecognition at the consummation of history.

By this close attachment of the consummation of all things to the present, Jesus infused his teachings with an eternal quality that gives to them an urgency and an importance which they could not have otherwise. It is well for the interpreter and student to grasp the significance of this method of Jesus. It was by design that Jesus intermingled the eschatological with the present, for by this intermingling Jesus lifted his teachings above the restrictions of his own age, or any age, and made them universal and eternal. By keeping before his disciples the consummation of all things while emphasizing the importance of obedience to his teachings in the present, Jesus intended to show that the teachings are validated in the eternal purposes of God and that they are therefore of immense importance. Contrary to the view of Schweitzer, the emphasis of Jesus upon eschatology does not confine the relevancy of his ethical teachings to the lifetime of Jesus. (See his *The Quest of the Historical Jesus,* p. 352.) Rather does this emphasis give to his ethical teachings an eternal quality and a universal significance they would not otherwise have.

We pass now to a study of the "Little Apocalypse."

VIII. The Son of Man in the "Little Apocalypse"

(Mark 13:1-37; Matthew 24:1-42; Luke 21:5-36)

This eschatological discourse of Jesus was precipitated by the remark of the disciples concerning the stones and the building of the Temple and the reply of Jesus that "there shall not be left one stone upon another, that shall not be thrown down." It was this remark that inspired four of the disciples (Peter, James, John, and Andrew) to go to Jesus privately and ask, according to Mark, "Tell us when shall these things be, and what shall be the sign when these things are all about to be accomplished?" Matthew records that the disciples also requested Jesus to inform them concerning the *Parousia* and the *consummation of the age.* The request, according to Matthew, was, "Tell us, when shall these things (i.e., the destruction of the Temple) be? And what the sign of thy coming (*Parousia*), and of the consummation of the age (*sunteleias tou aiōnas*)." In Matthew's account Jesus untertakes to inform the disciples as to these three events: (1) the destruction of the Temple; (2) the *Parousia;* (3) the consummation of the age (not the "end of the world").

Jesus begins by warning the disciples against being led astray by false Christs and by "wars and rumors of wars." The latter are the "beginnings of travail." He then proceeds to tell of the persecutions that are in store for them, and Mark records that he said, "And the gospel must first be preached unto all the nations"(v. 10). Then comes the prediction of the divisions to take place in families and the suffering and hatred in store for the followers of Jesus. All these things are to take place before the destruction of the Temple, for it is only after these predictions that the sign of the destruction of the Temple and of the fall of Jerusalem is given. This is the presence of the "abomination of desolation," spoken of by Daniel, in the holy place of the

Temple (Mark 13:14; Matthew 24:15). When this sign is seen, the disciples are to make every effort to escape from Jerusalem. Detailed instructions are given by Jesus for the conduct of his followers when this terrible event takes place (Mark 13:14-23; Matthew 24:15-28; Luke 21:20-24). These instructions are suggestive, not only of the thoughtfulness and kindness of Jesus, but also of his practical foresight. There was no advantage to be gained for the progress of the gospel in the needless slaughter of his followers in the terrible holocaust that would take place when Jerusalem fell before an invading army. Jesus again warns against the appearance of false Christs. They and the false prophets will arise to seize upon this event as a sign of Christ's coming. In effect Jesus says, "Pay no attention to them." His words concerning these apocalyptists are: "And then if any man shall say to you, Lo, here is Christ (*the* Christ—*ho Christos*); or, lo, he is there; believe him not." (The apocalyptists have used wars and world-shaking events ever since to lead people astray concerning the "coming" of Christ.) The aim of these false prophets and false Christs would be to "lead astray, if possible, the elect." According to Matthew, Jesus warns that the destruction of the Temple and the fall of Jerusalem thus described are not the sign of the *Parousia* of the Son of Man. His words are: "For as the lightning cometh out of the east, and shineth even unto the west; so shall also the coming [*Parousia*] of the Son of man be" (24:27). Up to now Jesus has answered the inquiry of the disciples concerning the destruction of the Temple, and he has answered the question concerning the sign of the *Parousia* to the extent that he has declared that the destruction of the Temple and the fall of Jerusalem *will not be a sign of the Parousia.* There yet remains an answer to the question concerning the consummation of the age, and more is to be said about the *Parousia.*

The most difficult part of the prophecy of Jesus comes now. It is introduced with these words in Mark's version: "But in those days, after that tribulation, the sun shall be darkened, and the moon shall not give her light, and the stars of heaven shall fall, and the powers that are in heaven shall be shaken. And then shall they see the Son of man coming (*erchomenon*) in the clouds with great power and glory. And then shall he send his angels, and shall gather together his elect from the four winds, from the uttermost part of the earth to the uttermost part of heaven."

This statement brings us to the crucial point of the whole discussion. If by these words Jesus was predicting his *Parousia*—what is popularly known as his *second coming*—then he was an apocalyptist who erred grievously in his prophecy, for all three Synoptic writers agree that Jesus said in connection with this prophecy, "Verily I say unto you, that this generation shall not pass, till all these things be done [accomplished]" (Mark 13:30; Matthew 24:34; Luke 21:32). We know also that there was no literal fulfilment of the prophecy by Jesus concerning cosmic disturbances. We are compelled to admit either that Jesus made a grievous blunder in his prediction of his "coming" immediately after the destruction of Jerusalem, (in which case we are also compelled to admit that he was a thorough-going apocalyptist), or that he employed apocalyptic language to describe, not his *Parousia* but a "coming" of another sort. The truth lies with the latter alternative. This "coming" of the Son of Man "in the clouds with great power and glory" could not have been a reference to the *Parousia;* the word *parousia* is not used to describe it; it is a "coming" that took place after the destruction of the Jewish theocratic state with the demolition of the Temple and the fall of Jerusalem in A.D. 70. In describing this "coming" Jesus gave the disciples an answer to their inquiry concerning the "consummation of the age." The destruction of the Temple and the end of the Jewish theocratic state, with this "coming" of the Son of Man, did indeed mark the consummation of an age.

The evidence for the view that this "coming" of the Son of Man "in the clouds with great power and glory" is not a reference to the *Parousia* is close at hand. It is first of all the clear statement of Jesus: "But of that day and that hour knoweth no man, no, not the angels which are in heaven, *neither the Son,* but the Father." It would be strange indeed if this remark applied to that "coming" of the Son of Man "in the clouds with great power and glory" that Jesus foretold would take place *in those days, after that tribulation* (the tribulation connected with the fall of Jerusalem). According to Matthew Jesus said, "*Immediately* after the tribulation of those days shall the sun be darkened, et cetera . . . And then shall appear the sign of the Son of man in heaven . . . and they shall see the Son of Man coming in the clouds of heaven with power and great glory." Jesus could hardly have been more specific in locating the time of this coming. It would be "*in those days, after that tribulation,*" or as Matthew has it, "*immediately after the tribulation of those days.*" And yet Jesus declared that even the Son was in ignorance of *that day and hour.* This declaration of ignorance applies not merely to the time but to signs of the day's approach and to what is to take place when the day comes. This is apparent from the manner in which the statement is made—"But of that day and that hour knoweth no man"; the statement is correctly rendered, "*Concerning* that day or that hour," since the Greek preposition is *peri.* Thus "the *time* of that day or that hour" does not correctly convey the meaning. Jesus was saying that men, angels, and even the Son were in ignorance of the time, nature, and accompanying signs of this day of which he speaks. How, then, could this disclaimer of knowledge apply to the "coming" of the Son of Man "in the clouds with great power and glory," a "coming" the time of which Jesus definitely fixed and the accompanying signs of which he described in detail? It could not, and careful attention to this context will show that it could apply only to the *Parousia,* which is introduced by Jesus at this point in order that he may answer the inquiry the disciples made in the beginning with reference to the "sign of thy coming [*Parousia*]" (Matthew 24:3).

In Mark that part of Jesus' conversation dealing with things to come is ended very abruptly with this disclaimer of knowledge concerning "that day or that hour." In the Greek "that day or that hour" is a very definite phrase: *tēs hēmeras ekeinēs ē tēs hōras,* indicating that the day and hour referred to are set over in contrast with the days that are described immediately preceding this point. To render properly in English, we would say, "But of *that* day or *that* hour knoweth no man," etc. It is not, "But of that *day* or that *hour* knoweth no man," etc. Hence the reference is to a day or hour that was not under immediate discussion and is not applicable in Mark, which does not use the word *parousia* at this point, to the "coming" of the Son of Man "in the clouds with great power and glory."

Matthew clinches the evidence for our view here, however, by his use of the term *parousia.* His statement is: "But of that day and hour knoweth no man, no, not the angels of heaven, but my Father only. But as the days of Noah were, so shall also the coming [*parousia*] of the Son of man be" (24:36f.). Jesus then proceeds, *not to give any sign that would indicate the time of the Parousia,* but to show that *there will be no extraordinary events to signalize it.* Just as men were eating, drinking, marrying and giving in marriage up until the day that Noah entered the ark, so men will be going about their accustomed pursuits when the *Parousia* takes place—"so shall also the coming [*parrousia*] of the Son of man be" (24:39). This will be the day of final separation between the righteous and the unrighteous—"Then shall two be in the field; the one shall be taken, and the other left" (24:40). "Watch, therefore," Jesus warns, *"for ye know not what hour your Lord doth come"* (24:42).

We see, therefore, that, contrary to popular notions, Jesus gave no signs whatever concerning his "Second Coming." He specifically disclaimed knowledge concerning this coming—*the Parousia.* He predicted that there would be a *Parousia,* a "Second Coming," if it must be called by that name, declared that men would be engaged in the ordinary pursuits of life when it took place, warned his followers to be ready for the great event, and left the matter there.

There are those who would raise the question here as to the capacity of Jesus to foresee and in some measure describe the fall of Jerusalem. The question presents no problem to those who ascribe to Jesus the power of divine foresight. However, it is possible to leave aside the ascription of this power to Jesus and yet understand how it would be possible for one endowed with the insight and wisdom he possessed to foresee the end of the Jewish state. He was fully aware of the political and spiritual movements of his time. It would be entirely possible for him to foresee the inevitable disaster that awaited the Jewish nation because of the growing nationalism that placed it in an increasingly antagonistic attitude toward Rome. But more keenly than his awareness of this cause of the approaching disaster would be his consciousness of the terrible portent of disaster visible in the blind refusal of the religious leaders to accept his way of salvation. This refusal he saw as the chief cause of the coming storm that would destroy the edifice of Israel. The power to foresee the inevitable working out of the unchangeable laws of the spiritual universe belonged to Jesus in an exceptional degree. Men of prophetic instinct and lofty spiritual endowment possess it in a lesser degree. As an illustration of the possession of this power the case of Woodrow Wilson may be cited. He foresaw and predicted another great world war that would come as a result of developing isolationism in the United States after the close of World War I in 1918. We may be sure that the human and divine gifts of Jesus enabled him to foresee with greater accuracy the disaster that would overtake his nation.

This brings us back to a brief consideration of one or two problems connected with the prediction of Jesus concerning that other "coming," the "coming" of the Son of Man "in the clouds with great power and glory" after the destruction of the Temple and the fall of Jerusalem. The first of these is the question as to whether or not we are justified in referring the prediction of Jesus concerning the celestial disturbances that would take place (the darkening of the sun, the failing of the moon, the falling of the stars) to a "coming" of Jesus that would be spiritual in nature and unaccompanied by actual cosmic disturbances. Still another question is, Why should Jesus use such apocalyptic language to describe a "coming" of the Son of Man or of the coming of the Kingdom "in power" after the fall of Jerusalem? And yet another question that demands answer is, What was the nature of this "coming" of the Son of Man that was to take place after the fall of Jerusalem?

The first question as to whether we are justified in giving a spiritual and nonliteral interpretation to these predictions of Jesus is answered in part by the manner in which Peter applied a prophecy couched in apocalyptic terms on the day of Pentecost. It will be remembered that when Peter rose to explain the extraordinary manifestations of the Spirit he said, "This is that which was spoken by the prophet Joel." He then goes on to quote from Joel: "And I will show wonders in heaven above, and signs in the earth beneath; blood, and fire, and vapour of smoke: The sun shall be turned into darkness, and the moon into blood, before that great and notable day of the Lord come" (Acts 2:16, 19f.). The point here is that Peter applied this prophecy, filled with apocalyptic imagery descriptive of cosmic disturbances, to the day of Pentecost and the events that were then transpiring. *"This is that which was spoken by the prophet Joel,"* Peter said. Peter's application of apocalyptic imagery in a nonliteral way to spiritual events should strongly suggest that Jesus might likewise have employed apocalyptic language to foretell the happening of spiritual events and that in its use neither Jesus nor the disciples understood that literal fulfilment of the predictions was expected. Here is evidence that Jesus transformed the apocalypticism of the first century by applying it to spiritual events and that his effort in this direction was in some measure successful.

But why should Jesus choose this method of foretelling the "coming" of the Son of Man and of the Kingdom in power? Several reasons suggest themselves: (1) He wished to impress upon the minds of the disciples with unforgettable symbolism the extraordinary nature of the events of the period through which they would pass when the Temple was destroyed and a new day of opportunity for the Kingdom dawned. (2) He wished to assure them by use of this exalted symbolism of the sure and certain presence of God's hand in history in spite of the disaster that would come to the Jewish state—Jerusalem might fall, but that only meant the "coming" of the Son of Man in glory and of the Kingdom in power. He wanted them to be prepared for this great crisis by foreknowledge of it—prepared for the suffering, but prepared also for the onward march of the Son of Man in history. (3) By reference to the darkening of the sun, the failing of the moon to give her light, and the falling of the stars from heaven, it is quite possible that Jesus wished to leave with the disciples a prediction of the "fall" of world rulers and world powers before the onward march of his gospel in view of the fact that in apocalyptic literature heavenly bodies are used to designate kings and rulers and great personages. It would be the part of wisdom that such predictions were veiled, since by their repetition in direct form harm might come to the followers of Christ.

The question that remains concerns the actual meaning of this coming of the Son of Man that was to follow the fall of Jerusalem. The question is partially answered in what has been said, but a further word is necessary. By this "coming" we understand that Jesus meant that the end of the Jewish theocratic state and the abolition of Temple worship would signalize the emergence of his gospel as a real factor in history. Here would begin the triumphant march of the Son of Man in history; here would begin the real rise of the Kingdom of God in power. Concerning the prediction of the sending forth by the Son of Man of his angels to "gather together his elect from the four winds, from the uttermost part of the earth to the uttermost part of heaven" (Mark 13:27), this may well be applied to the conversion of men of every nation to the gospel, men who by becoming disciples of the Kingdom are numbered with the elect. This "gathering of the elect" is now in progress and will continue until the *Parousia*.

IX. The Day of the Son of Man in Luke 17:20-37

This passage, though showing similarities with the "Little Apocalypse," is peculiar to Luke and must be assigned to *L*, his special source.

It is recorded in Luke 17:20 that the Pharisees asked Jesus, "When comes the kingdom of God?" The reply of Jesus was, "The kingdom of God cometh not with observation: neither shall they say, Lo here! or lo there! for, behold the kingdom of God is within you."

These words deal a blow to the Schweitzer-Dispensationalist theory of the Kingdom in the statement of Jesus, "The kingdom of God cometh not with observation." If the Kingdom was an apocalyptic affair to come in suddenly and to be established in Palestine during the lifetime of Jesus, as according to Schweitzer it was in the thinking of Jesus, how could Jesus say, "The kingdom of God cometh not with observation"? And if, as the Dispensationalists claim, the Kingdom is that kingdom which is to be set up upon the earth when Jesus returns, how could he say, "The kingdom of God cometh not with observation"? Certainly in the theory of Schweitzer and the Dispensationalists the Kingdom is something tangible, something that can be observed, a kingdom that may be pointed to by men who say, "Lo, here! or, lo there!" (that is, "Here it is!" or, "There it is!")

But the words of Jesus deliver another telling blow to the materialistic conception of the Kingdom held by Schweitzer and the Dispensationalists. Jesus says, "The kingdom of God is within you."

There is difference of opinion as to the meaning of the word *entos,* translated here "within." It is the opinion of the writer that it cannot mean "in the midst." In the latest edition of Lidell and Scott's Lexicon there is not a single citation to a classic author who uses the word in this sense. A reference is given in which the *entos* means "the inner parts" (of the body). The word seems to be a strengthened form of the preposition *en,* like our *within.* It undoubtedly emphasizes the *inner* nature of something. Its use here emphasizes the inner and spiritual nature of the Kingdom; by its use the Gospel writer records Jesus as setting forth the Kingdom of God as an unseen but spiritual realm which was being realized and actualized in the minds and hearts of living individuals.

The objection is raised to this interpretation that Jesus

was speaking to the Pharisees and could not have meant that the Kingdom of God was *within* them. (But E. Stanley Jones thinks that Jesus did mean that the Kingdom of God was *in* the Pharisees! See his book, *Is The Kingdom of God Realism?* p. 73.) Of course Jesus could not have meant that the Kingdom of God was *in* these Pharisees to whom he was speaking. These words are the statement of a universal proposition. The same type of statement in English is well understood as a universal proposition. A minister addressing a group of unbelievers might say, "The love of God is within you," meaning not that the love of God was within those to whom he was speaking, but that the love of God is a power capable of being realized in the hearts of all men. This objection to the interpretation of *entos* as *within* may therefore be dismissed as not having sufficient weight, and we may with confidence believe that the use of the word emphasizes the invisible and spiritual nature of the Kingdom.

It is this very invisible and spiritual nature of the Kingdom, however, that assures its universality and reality. If it is only apocalyptic and eschatological in nature, as Schweitzer and Dispensationalists say that it is, then it is not universal and neither is it a reality. It is not universal in that it is limited to the apocalyptic delusion of Jesus on the one hand, or to the period following the Second Coming on the other; it is not real, because in Schweitzer's view it was never realized in history, whereas according to Dispensationalists it cannot be realized until Jesus comes again.

The answer of Jesus to the question of the Pharisees precludes limitation of the Kingdom of God to apocalypticism, and at the same time reveals its spiritual, universal, and real nature. The Kingdom, by Jesus' statement, must be understood as the reign of God, the moral and spiritual realm in which the will of God prevails. As such it may be described as the *dominion* of God. In that it is *within* you it is capable of realization in human experience and on the plane of human history. It is real and present because it may be incarnated in living individuals and in groups of living men and women. The Kingdom IS, not *was* or *will be,* in this statement of Jesus; that is to say, it is *eternal.* We should not speak of "bringing it in"; rather should we say, "Let it in!"

This brings us to the consideration of the relation of the Kingdom to the Day of the Son of Man. Jesus was aware of the confusion that was likely to arise in the minds of his disciples in connection with a question concerning the Kingdom. Following his reply to the question of the Pharisees, he directs his attention to the disciples and proceeds to teach them concerning the Great Day in which the Son of Man will be "revealed." This we take to be the day of the *Parousia.* He had plainly taught that the Kingdom is *present*; he proceeds to show that the *Parousia* is *to be.* Thus does he place the *Parousia* in its proper temporal relation to the Kingdom. It is more proper to say that having shown that the Kingdom is *eternal,* he proceeds to reveal that the *Parousia* is temporal. He said to the disciples, "The days will come, when ye shall desire to see one of the days [as the translations have it] of the Son of man, and ye shall not see it."

A common misunderstanding of this verse is that the disciples, in the future, after Jesus is taken away from them, will remember with longing the happy days they spent with their Master in Galilee and will meditate with nostalgic satisfaction upon the joy that would be theirs if they could but spend one of those days with him again. But such an interpretation fails to meet the demands of the context, not to mention the fact that Jesus would hardly have wasted time in dignifying any purely sentimental and human emotions which his disciples might entertain concerning him to the point of making them the subject of a moral discourse. The statement of Jesus concerning the desire of the disciples to see "one" of the days of the Son of Man must be referred to the future, not to the past.

But why should Jesus speak of the disciples as longing to see *one* of the days of the Son of Man? What is to be made of this expression, "*one* of the days of the Son of Man?" We believe that the answer is to be found in a different rendering of the word translated here as "one."

Let the word be rendered *first* and the mystery is at once cleared up. The Greek word is *mian,* the accusative feminine of the cardinal *heis,* meaning *one.* The cardinal *heis* in the feminine (*mia*) occurs in certain places in the sense in which the ordinal is used, namely, *first.* In 1 Corinthians 16:2 Paul says, "Upon the first day of the week let each one of you lay by him in store, et cetera." The word for *first* here is *mian,* and it is difficult to see how any other meaning can be given *mian* in this sentence except *first.* In Acts 20:7 *En de tē mia tōn sabbatōn* is, "And upon the first day of the week", et cetera. Once again the only probable meaning of *mia* is *first,* not *one.* In these two passages, and in Luke 17:22, the emphasis on *first* is not the time element, but the element of priority. The *first* day of the week was in fact the first in point of time, but as the "Lord's day" (Revelation 1:10—*kuriakē hemerē*) it was first in importance, the *chief* day. Hence the *Parousia* is the chief of the days of the Son of Man.

Thus the statement of Jesus to the disciples is, "The days will come when ye shall desire to see the *chief* of the days of the Son of Man, and ye shall not see it." The meaning of the statement is that the disciples will long to see the *Parousia* of the Son of Man and shall not see it. The implication in the warning is that disciples in times of future tribulation will long to be delivered by the sudden coming of the Son of Man. The following verse suggests that they will be tempted to give credence to announcements that the Son of Man has come or is about to come. "And they shall say to you, See here; or, see there," warns Jesus. But the disciples are not to listen to the false prophets; they themselves will be able to recognize without any doubt the signs of the coming. Even as the lightning flashing in one part of the heavens lights up the other part of the heavens, "so shall also the Son of man be in his day." It is worthy of note that the singular *his day* occurs in this last statement, thus corroborating the rendering of *mian* in verse 22 as the *first* or the *chief* of the days. Thus Jesus promises that the Great Day will come, but he warns his followers against being misled by those who would make claims of superior knowledge concerning the coming of the Day.

The warning of Jesus is suggestive in the light of the tendency of Christian groups through the centuries to revive apocalyptic hopes in times of upheaval, war, and persecution. Those who long for the Day may not see it, even as the early disciples longed for it and did not see it. Others may be tempted to follow after the Dispensationalists who say, "See here; or, see there." They should remember the admonition of Jesus, "Go not after them, nor follow them."

If *mian* be taken as the *chief* of the days of the Son of Man in verse 22, then the *days* of the Son of Man in verse 26 may be interpreted with a measure of satisfaction. In verse 25 Jesus predicts that his suffering and death must precede the Day of the Son of Man. His rejection, he says, will be by "this generation," but he does not say that the *Parousia* will immediately follow the rejection. Now he proceeds to say, "And as it came to pass in the days of Noah, even so shall it be also in the days of the Son of man. They were eating, they were drinking, they were marrying, they were giving in marriage [these are imperfects], until the day that Noah entered into the ark, and the flood came, and destroyed them all." A similar statement follows concerning the "days of Lot." Now it is evident that if the days of Noah are to be a true figure of the days of the Son of Man, the "days" of the Son of Man must precede the Day (that is, the *Parousia*) of the Son of Man, for with the onset of the flood the eating, the drinking, the marrying, and the giving in marriage were suddenly terminated, and we are bound to conclude that Jesus meant that in like manner the eating, the drinking, the marrying, and the giving in marriage of "the days" of the Son of Man would be as suddenly terminated with the coming of the Son of Man in "his day." If the figure is to hold, it is necessary for the flood and the salvation of Noah by the ark in verse 27, and the destruction of Sodom and the salvation of Lot in verse 29 to symbolize the Day of the Son of Man. Just as the destruction of Sodom put an end to the drinking, the buying, the selling, the planting of Lot's day, so the *Parousia* of the Son of Man will put an end to the drinking, buying, selling, planting, and building in another period. This drinking, buying, selling, planting, building must therefore come *before* the Day of the Son of Man, hence, must take place during the *days* of the Son of Man. These *days* of the Son of Man can be no other than the days in which we are now living, the days that have come and gone since the crucifixion and resurrection of Jesus, the days that will continue to come and go until the Son of Man returns in his *Parousia.* The Day of the Son of Man, the *chief* day of verse 22, the *day* of verses 24, 30-31, is the climactic day that will terminate the *days* of the Son of Man. When the Day comes, people will be found as indifferent and as deeply immersed in material affairs as they were in the days of Noah and in the days of Lot. Even as the day of the flood and the day of the destruction of Sodom were days of calamity for the unrighteous, so the Day of the Son of Man will be a day of calamity for the unrighteous; but even as the day of the flood and the day of the destruction of Sodom were days of deliverance for Noah and for Lot, so the Day of the Son of Man will be a day of deliverance and salvation for the people of God.

Jesus now tells of preparation for the Great Day. Let a man so live that when the Great Day comes he will not desire to rush from his housetop to secure his earthly treasure that is within his house (v. 31). Let him not be attached to the things of the earth in such a fashion that he could not gladly be separated from them at a moment's notice. Let him lose his life if he would bring it forth alive (*zōogonēsei*) (v. 33). The Day will be a day of separation because some are prepared for it, others are not (vv. 34-35).

The disciples had a final question. They asked, "Where Lord?" meaning, "Where are all these things to take place?" The reply of Jesus was, "Wheresoever the body is, thither will the eagles [birds of carrion, vultures] be gathered together." By this Jesus meant to say that all these things would take place wherever the dead carcass of sinning humanity was to be found, which was a way of saying that they would take place everywhere, since sinners would be found the world over.

"The kingdom of God is *within* you." The Kingdom therefore is spiritual and real—it is HERE and NOW! The Great Day of the Son of Man is a day in time. Concerning it be not deceived, but for it prepare! We now live in the days of the Son of Man. These will be terminated by the *Parousia,* the Great Day of the Son of Man which is yet to come.

This is the teaching of Jesus.

In good conscience, therefore, and in the knowledge that abundant evidence supports the view, we conclude that Jesus was no apocalyptist in his use of the title Son of Man. Thus it has been possible to trace one of the two important ways in which the title underwent transformation in its use by Jesus. The other, having to do with his addition to the Son of Man concept of the idea of the Suffering Servant, is now before us.

V

CAESAREA PHILIPPI

2. *From Death to Life*

The Son of Man is the Suffering Servant. This is the amazing revelation that Jesus makes after hearing from the lips of Peter that he is the Christ, the Son of the living God. According to Mark, "he began to teach them, that the Son of man must suffer many things, and be rejected of the elders and of the chief priests, and scribes, and be killed, and after three days rise again" (8:31). Matthew says, "*From that time* began Jesus *Christ* [the best texts add Christ] to show unto his disciples, how that he must go unto Jerusalem, and suffer many things of the elders and chief priests and scribes, and be killed, and be raised again the third day" (16:21). By the addition of the significant phrase *from that time* Matthew indicates that this is the beginning of a new and revolutionary phase in the ministry of Jesus. It is the opening of that phase that points wholly in the direction of his death. From now on everything in the ministry of Jesus, teaching and activity, will shape itself around that sad but climactic event on Calvary. Matthew, by his use of the term Jesus *Christ*, points to the fact that it is the Messiah who now makes the astounding revelation that he is to be rejected and killed. In the mind of Jesus it is peculiarly the Son of Man who faces rejection and death. In the accounts of both Mark and Luke it is in the content of Jesus' teaching that the *Son* of *Man* must suffer and be rejected and killed. (Mark 8:31; Luke 9:22). Here, then, at Caesarea Philippi, Jesus reveals the extraordinary synthesis in his own person of the Son of Man and the Suffering Servant; here he shows the revolutionary transformation that had taken place in the concept of the Son of Man, as it passed through the crucible of his mind and soul. Not only had he stripped the Son of Man of his apocalyptic trappings, he had now brought him to the lowly threshold of suffering and death, so that the Mighty One conceived of by Daniel as "coming with the clouds of heaven" might also be Isaiah's Suffering One who would be "wounded for our transgressions" and "bruised for our iniquities."

There need not be too much wonder at the amazement with which this extraordinary revelation was received by Simon Peter. If Peter knew anything at all about the Son of Man, he knew him as the great supernatural personage of the apocalyptic writings. His conception of the Messiah was at this time quite similar to that held by the people at large. The Messiah of popular expectation was likewise a great personage—one who would restore the kingdom of David, destroy the enemies of Jehovah, and set up the great kingdom of righteousness. It was inconceivable that to be rejected and die was any part of this Messiah's mission. Peter had just confessed Jesus as the Messiah and had heard his Master pronounce him blessed because he made the confession; often he had heard Jesus refer to himself as Son of Man, and now again at Caesarea Philippi he hears him use the majestic title in referring to himself. It is not to be wondered at, therefore, that when Jesus began to tell his disciples that he who called himself the Son of Man, and who was confessed by them as the Messiah, was to be rejected and killed by the religious leaders, the announcement was like a bolt of lightning from the clouds that struck them into amazed incredulity. Peter gave voice to the sentiment of all when after taking Jesus aside (see Mark 8:32f.) he said (literally), "Mercy on thee, Lord, by no means shall this be unto thee" (Matthew 16:22). It was simply inconceivable to these men that rejection and death at the hands of the religious leaders of the nation could be the lot of him whom they had come to believe was the Christ, the Son of the living God. It would have been far more agreeable to their mode of thinking had Jesus revealed to them the fact that the time had come for him to go to Jerusalem and publicly announce the restoration of the Davidic throne and call for the support of the religious leaders in placing him thereon.

The reaction of Jesus to Peter's remonstrance is indicative of the immensity and depth of the conviction at which he had arrived concerning his approaching death. There leaps from his lips a sentence that is like a dart from the depths of a cauldron of fire, pointed with flame that will sear and burn as it falls upon the ears of those who stand by and listen in paralyzed amazement. It is directed toward the man who has just risen to heights to confess his Master as the Christ and who has received from him the accolade: "Blessed art thou, Simon Barjona . . . thou art *Petros.*" Surely these sharp, burning words from Jesus' lips betray no shallow emotionalism concerning a decision lightly or recently made; surely they reveal a conviction so deep and unshakable that its only explanation could be that its source was in the very fiber of the character of him who gave expression to it. "Get thee behind me, Satan: for thou mindest not the things that be of God, but the things that be of men." These are the words that fall upon the ears of the startled man who only a few short minutes before had heard from the same lips, "Blessed art thou, Simon Barjona . . . thou art *Petros.*"

Why does Jesus see Peter stand here as Satan's representative when the spokesman of the twelve remonstrates with his Master concerning the announced necessity of his death at Jerusalem? It was because Jesus now saw his death as an expression of the character and will of God. "Thou art an offence [a *skandalon,* a stumblingblock] unto me," said Jesus: "for thou mindest not the things that be of God, but those that be of men." Peter was now like a stone in the pathway of Jesus, not *Petros* for the foundation of the *ekklēsia,* because he was attempting to block the execution of God's will. Peter was now the voice of Satan and was speaking the language of men because the Messiah whom he visualized was bedecked with the trappings of the world. This thing that he was saying, unlike his good confession of Jesus as the Christ, was not the result of a revelation from the Father. Peter was now minding the "things that be of men."

Why did Jesus deem it necessary to go to Jerusalem and die? Here in part is the answer in these harsh words of Jesus to Peter. That Peter was not "minding the things that be of God" in his remonstrance with Jesus speaks eloquently of the conviction of Jesus that his death belonged to those "things that be of God." Here we discover that his death had become for Jesus the great divine imperative; it would be for him the expression of God's will. From this point on he begins to show his disciples "how that he *must* go unto Jerusalem, and suffer many things of the elders and chief priests and scribes, and be killed, and be raised again the third day." There is now upon him a powerful constraint—he *must* go to Jerusalem and die.

Jesus bases the necessity for his death, as this conversation shows, in the character and will of God. It is the character and will of God that make his death the great imperative of his life. As the Son of God Jesus can do no other than reveal the true character of God the Father. At the age of twelve he knew God in a unique sense as Father; in the wilderness temptation the manner of the approaches of Satan, "if thou art the Son of God," indicated the consciousness then of his Sonship. At Caesarea Philippi he accepts Peter's confession that he is the Son of the living God. He knows God as Father—he knows him therefore as the God of redeeming love. As the Son he must manifest him as such because he is the Son. But why must he die in order to reveal him as Father and as love? This is because his death must be the inevitable result of the conflict between love and sin. Jesus knows that when love and sin meet, love can have but one answer: *love.*

This revelation of his impending death shows that Jesus is aware of the rising tide of sin against him. He has seen this tide in the envy and hatred of the religious leaders; he knows that it will engulf him in the end. When the evil men who even now seek his destruction reach out sinful hands to pull him down, what will be his answer? He knows there can be but one answer: love. He cannot answer hate with hate, force with force, because he is the Son of God the Father, the Father who is love. What then will be his pattern? Not that of the mighty conquering Messiah who could call legions of angels to his defense, but the lowly Servant of whom Isaiah sang when he said, "He was oppressed, and he was afflicted, yet he opened not his mouth: he is brought as a lamb to the slaughter, and as a sheep before her shearers is dumb, so he opened not his mouth." It was this Suffering Servant who would reveal the answer of redeeming love to sin manifested as hatred and cruelty; it was this Suffering Servant who would show the character of God the Father.

At this point where redeeming love collides with sin Jesus knows that atonement for the sins of men will be wrought out. He will say in a short while as he endeavors to bring the twelve closer to the meaning of his death: "the Son of man came not to be ministered unto, but to minister and to give his life a ransom for many" (Mark 10:45; Matthew 20:28). What is this *ransom* for many that he says his life will be? The Greek word is *lutron.* It was used of the payment that a slave would make to secure his own freedom. It represented that which was given in exchange for the life of the slave—that which by being given secured the slave's release from bondage. Jesus sees his death in this light. The giving of his life will be the ransom price that will secure the release of the many. Israel is in his mind as he thinks of himself, Israel's Messiah, as paying a ransom price that the nation may be saved. But all men are in his mind, for he will pay this price as the great Son of Man; the ransom will be universal in its efficacy—it will be for all. Again he sees himself as the Suffering Servant. He will be the one of whom Isaiah said: "But he was wounded for our transgressions, he was bruised for our iniquities: the chastisement of our peace was upon him; and with his stripes we are healed. All we like sheep have gone astray; we have turned every one to his own way; and the Lord hath laid on him the iniquity of us all."

Isaiah had seen the great truth of atonement. One great one who should come must die lest all die. Man's sin was great but man was small. Who was man that he could render to God that which was necessary to satisfy the holiness of God? And yet God was love—would he destroy man? No, God would give to man a Servant who would suffer in man's stead; one who in his person would satisfy the holiness of God and reveal the love of God the Father. Such an one would be "despised and rejected of men; a man of sorrows, and acquainted with grief," but he would "see of the travail of his soul" and "be satisfied" because of him Jehovah could say "by his knowledge shall my righteous servant justify many; for he shall bear their iniquities."

The mystery of atonement is great, but Jesus saw it clearly, saw it like Isaiah saw it, as the only solution of the problem of sin. He saw himself as the great Son of Man capable of providing universal atonement by fulfilling the qualifications of the Suffering Servant revealed in Isaiah's matchless poem. He knew that in his acceptance of death at the hands of the religious leaders of the nation he would unveil forever the heart of God so that man might henceforth see that in the heart of God there was redeeming love. Would not this be the only weapon that could ever be provided to break the heart of man and compel him to acknowledge his sins and seek forgiveness? To go to Jerusalem and announce himself as the great Messiah who had come to restore David's throne—could this save Israel? No! Even were he to throw off Rome's yoke and establish a kingdom of righteousness, this could last only for a generation and provide security for a few million Jews for only a few brief years. To resist the evil men when they seized him, to organize his followers and effect a *coup* that would save his own life and free the multitudes from oppression at the hands of the corrupt leaders—could this save Israel or provide salvation for the many? No! Men would fight and die in the conflict—this would be the way of sin, not the way of love. No, love dictated but one course—that was the course of acceptance of rejection and death. He must go to Jerusalem as the Suffering Servant of Jehovah.

Was it necessary to go on to Jerusalem? Might he not live on in Galilee, live on and do the works of the Christ? Live on and heal the blind, cleanse the lepers, preach good news to the poor? live on and sow the seed of the Kingdom? No, there was no escaping Jerusalem! The love of God must be revealed there. At Jerusalem the revelation of his Messiahship must be made to the nation. At Jerusalem, the heart and center of Israel, only at Jerusalem, could the demonstration of his complete fulfilment of prophecy be made. Only at Jerusalem could he officially reveal himself as the Messiah, the Son of God, the Son of Man, the Suffering Servant of Jehovah. Jerusalem was the seat of Israel's king—there must Israel's true king be made known. He could not escape Jerusalem and be true to himself and to God his Father.

This revelation that he is the Suffering Servant is another demonstration of the consistency of Jesus and of the integrity of his character. When in the wilderness of Judea he rejected the proposal to transform stones into bread, and when later he refused to defy natural law and cast himself from the pinnacle of the Temple, he accepted the limitations of the flesh and identified himself completely with the life of humanity. In this decision acceptance of suffering and death was implied—if not the manner of his death or its time. It was the challenge of sin expressed in the hatred and opposition of the religious leaders that brought Jesus to the crisis and revealed in sharp focus the necessity of his early rejection and death at Jerusalem.

From this point on Jesus would continue to warn his disciples that he must be rejected and die. On the Mount of Transfiguration Jesus and Peter, James and John would hear from heaven the Father's answer to the question: Who is this Son of Man who must suffer and die at Jerusalem? It was: "*This is my beloved Son: hear him.*"

The Way of the Cross for All

Out of the consciousness of the necessity and significance of his own death there came to Jesus the knowledge of a secret of supreme importance for all men: it was that *all men must die in order to live.* The revelation of this great principle follows immediately upon the revelation at Caesarea Philippi of his own impending death. The principle is so stated as to indicate the conviction of Jesus that it is universal in its application, that it is a law of the spiritual universe, certain and immutable in its operation. Again we see in an utterance of Jesus the reflection of an exalted conviction concerning his person and mission. Who but One who sustained a unique relationship to God; who but One who had searched the depths and heights of the spiritual universe; who but One who knew what was in man, would dare to say: *"Here is life's greatest secret—you must die in order to live"?* Surely he who dared to demand of men that they must die and claimed for himself the right to promise that for their dying they might live, conceived of himself as man's *One Saviour!*

It was the inevitable corollary to the revelation of his coming death that Jesus announced to the twelve: "If any man wishes to come after me, let him renounce himself, *and take up his cross*, and follow me." The words must have wrought dismay in the minds of the already sorely perplexed disciples. They had heard with consternation the words about his own approaching rejection and death; now they were hearing him say that every one of them would be compelled to take up a cross if he wished to follow on with Jesus. This was in effect an ultimatum, and it was doubtless so understood. These men who had left their occupations in Galilee to cast their lot with Jesus of Nazareth are now faced with a grave choice: they must accept the necessity of his death in Jerusalem, following him to the end, each accepting a cross for himself, or they must cease to be his disciples and turn back to their homes. Such was the crisis presented by the cross to the twelve when Jesus revealed the supreme test of discipleship in the regions of Caesarea Philippi. As the cross was the crisis for them, so it becomes the crisis for all men who would follow Jesus Christ and experience the living God through him. It is likely that the twelve wavered for a season. The faith of Peter, James, and John was fortified on the Mount of Transfiguration, but there is evidence that the twelve went to their own homes for a season before rejoining Jesus for the final journey to Jerusalem. In Matthew 17:22 the best texts read: "And while they were being *gathered together* [or *being re-united*] in Galilee," where the Authorized Version reads, "And while they abode in Galilee." Did they return to their homes to meditate upon the grave issue Jesus had presented to them? In any event, they came back to him to hear him repeat the unwelcome prediction of his death and proceeded with him on the last journey to Jerusalem. It is impossible to believe, however, that they comprehended the full import of his words until fifty and three days after he went to his cross, when the Holy Spirit came to interpret to them his death as their life and the cross that all of them must bear as the secret of experience with him.

What, then, did Jesus ask of these men when he demanded that every one of them must take up his own cross? They very well knew what a cross was. Execution by crucifixion was common in Galilee and all had doubtless witnessed the slow and terrible deaths of criminals condemned to die on Roman crosses. They understood the cross, therefore, as the symbol of public execution and death. Jesus chose the cross as the symbol of his demand in the knowledge that the twelve understood it as a symbol of crucifixion and death. But are we to understand that he was calling upon these men to go to Jerusalem and die with him? This could not be. The purpose of his ministry would have been defeated with the wholesale execution of the men to whom he had entrusted his gospel. Indeed Jesus himself interceded for the twelve with the soldiers who came to arrest him. In John's Gospel it is told that he said, "If therefore ye seek me, let these go their way" (18:8). No, these men were to live on beyond Calvary to tell the things they had seen and heard. But of more importance than the necessity for these men to live beyond Calvary was the fact that the cross of Peter, of James, of John, or the cross of any of the rest, was not the cross of Jesus Christ. The cross of Christ is what it is because it was Jesus, the Son of God, who died upon it, and the difference between the cross of Christ and the cross of Peter is the difference between Christ and Peter. In the cross of the Christ there is atonement for sins, because Christ is the universal Redeemer and Saviour; in the cross of the disciple there is crucifixion of self, but no atonement for the sins of others. Jesus did not demand of these men, therefore, that they die when he died, nor did he think of the cross of the disciples as equal with his own. How, then, are we to interpret his demand?

We must not seek escape from the truth the symbol of the cross imposes if we are sincere in our desire to know the demand Jesus makes. The cross is the symbol of death. In truth, then, Jesus requires that any man who would follow him must be willing to die for him; this is to say that the committal of the disciple to Jesus must be so irrevocable, so complete that the disciple would give his life, if his life be required of him, as evidence of his devotion. Jesus does not demand that every disciple be a martyr, though he asks that every disciple be a potential martyr; his demand was not designed to encourage martyrdom, but it will allow none who would follow Jesus to discount the possibility of martyrdom. Peter, James, John, Andrew, and perhaps others of the twelve, sealed their love for Christ by dying in his cause. All who would follow Jesus must be willing actually to lay down their lives for him. This is the inescapable import of Jesus' words. The willingness to die, to die even the public, disgraceful death which crucifixion imposed, is the proof of discipleship. What Jesus said to the twelve in the regions of Caesarea Philippi is meant for all who would follow him. His words were, "If *any man* wishes to come after me, let him renounce himself, and take up his cross, and follow me."

To take up one's cross and follow Jesus, then, is to commit oneself with utter devotion to Jesus and his way of life. How different is this from the popular conception of cross-bearing! There is a line in a well-known hymn that reflects the popular conception. It reads: "More strength to carry crosses I must bear." Crosses are here viewed as burdens, troubles, irritations. But this is a well-meaning perversion of the words of Jesus. Lines from another well-known hymn are more in keeping with the truth and spirit of what Jesus said. They are:

Must Jesus bear the cross alone,
And all the world go free?
No; There's a cross for every one,
And there's a cross for me.

This hymn is right because it does not speak of "crosses." Aside from the cross of Christ, there is but one cross for the individual who would follow Jesus—it is the cross of the crucifixion of his ego and the experience of utter surrender to Christ and to his way of life.

The substance of what we are saying is that the cross is a principle—a principle of living. Confession of Jesus as the Christ, the Son of the living God, is necessary, but it is not enough. It was not enough in the case of Peter and the twelve. Jesus added his death as essential to the office and work of the Christ, and the Christ becomes, therefore, the Christ of the Cross. If we confess him as the Christ, like the twelve we are faced with the necessity of accepting that which he adds as essential to the office and work of the Christ; or, failing to accept what he adds, we must turn back from following him. But if we accept the Christ of the Cross, then the cross as a way of life becomes our crisis and again there is no alternative to taking up our cross and following Jesus except rejecting him. Obedience to Christ, fellowship with Christ, following Christ—in short, true Christian experience is one with taking up a cross and following Jesus. It is this bearing of a cross that prevents the interpretation of Christianity as creed, or discipleship as belief. It is the bearing of a cross that compels us to translate what we believe about Jesus into experience; for he who is willing to seal his confession of Jesus as the Christ, the Son of the living God, with his own life's blood, is one to whom Jesus is in truth what he confesses him to be. The cross becomes for one who makes the good confession, then, the secret of his experience with Christ, the dynamic of his daily walk with the Son of God. When Jesus announced his approaching death, he also announced the principle of cross-bearing for all who would follow him. It is impossible, then, to separate the believer's cross from Christ's cross. In his way the believer must manifest the love of God through his cross as Jesus manifested the love of God through his cross. The cross of Christ and the cross of the believer have a common source: the love of God the Father. Christ's cross was the supreme manifestation of the Father's love; the cross of the believer is a lesser manifestation, but it is a manifestation of the same love. The cross of Christ is the heart of Christianity; the believer's cross is the medium through which the blood of Calvary is made effective in human experience. By crucifixion of the ego on his cross the believer destroys the shell of self that he may participate fully in the power of Calvary and enjoy union with Christ. Saul of Tarsus knew this secret and revealed it beautifully when he said, *"I am crucified with Christ; no longer I live, but Christ lives in me"* (Galatians 2:20).

The believer's cross is related in a very practical way to discipleship. Jesus was speaking to disciples when he announced the great principle of the cross at Caesarea Philippi, and he desired these men to continue as disciples. A disciple is a learner. A learner must believe his teacher, must accept the instruction of his teacher as truth, and must seek to make the contents of his teacher's instruction his own principles of conduct and living. Humility, an open mind, and confidence in the teacher are all essential qualities in the true disciple. Jesus is the great Teacher, we are the learners. Shall we accept his teachings, his ethical system, his principles of living? Pride and lack of faith in him move us to say, "Yes, with reservations." We are afraid some of his doctrines are too idealistic; we cannot see that it is possible to turn the other cheek and love one's enemies. Like Peter, we confess him as the Christ, the Son of the living God, but we are yet to face the crisis of a cross. But he replies to our confession: "I am the Christ of the cross. . . . Take up your cross and follow me." Only the crucifixion of our egos will make us true disciples—the ego must be slain, pride must go in order that we may say, "Yes, Lord, you have the words of life; we accept your teachings and your principles of living without reservation;—teach us, Lord, our minds are open."

The reward of obedience to the cross is life. Experience with God had taught Jesus that the gateway to life is death. He reveals the secret in his great paradox that follows his demand that every man who would come after him must renounce himself and take up his cross and follow him. The paradox is given as the explanation of the demand: "If anyone wishes to come after me, let him renounce himself and take up his cross and follow me; because whosoever would save his life shall lose it, but whosoever shall lose his life for my sake shall find it." We see here that Jesus equates the renunciation of self and the taking up a cross with the losing of one's life for Jesus' sake to find it. This confirms all we have said with respect to the meaning of the believer's cross, and there is no necessity to retrace our steps over familiar ground. Our effort must now be directed toward the understanding of the paradox. In it we believe Jesus gave expression to one of the profoundest truths in all history. It is so stated as to apply to all men; it must therefore be accepted, if we accept Jesus, as the statement of a supremely important universal truth, a truth that must demand the attention of all thinking men. Here is a categorical promise that every man who loses his life for the sake of Jesus will find his life. Two questions demand answer: (1) What is meant by a man's finding his life? (2) How does a man find his life by losing it for Jesus' sake?

The word translated *life* here is *psuchē,* which means *soul.* A man's soul is, in fact, his personality, his self. The promise, then, is that an individual who loses his life for Jesus' sake will find his *self,* his *personality.* Now there can be no doubt that Jesus is speaking here in terms of the eternal salvation of the soul, but it is just as true that he is also speaking of the fullest realization of selfhood in this present existence. An individual who finds his soul for eternity assuredly finds it in this present life. Jesus erected no barrier between life here and life beyond; indeed, he destroyed the barrier between life on earth and life to come. *Life in Christ is eternal life.* In this great paradox, then, Jesus reveals the secret of true self-realization. "Renounce self," says Jesus, "take up your cross, follow me, and you will become your best self." Jesus thus presents his way of life as the means of achieving maximum personality development. Everyone is compelled by Jesus to face his maximum possibilities as an individual created in the image of God, and is challenged to find his best self in discipleship to Jesus. Jesus does not promise to confer genius upon an individual, nor does he offer to make supermen of earth-bound individuals. The paradox takes account of differences in individual endowment; the promise is that whosoever shall lose *his* life for Jesus' sake will find *it*. Everyone is to find his own life, that is, the highest self of which he is capable. The promise is therefore reasonable, but its reasonableness in no wise diminishes its importance and significance for humanity. The average human being lives only half a life. The greatest down-drag to human progress is wasted and unused personality. Jesus measured men by their possibilities; and he saw infinite possibilities in every individual. He knew that he had discovered the secret whereby men might become their best selves; he revealed the secret to the twelve in the regions of Caesarea Philippi when he declared that a man finds his life by losing it.

We pass on to the second question raised by the paradox: How does a man find his life by losing it for Jesus' sake? We reply first by taking into account the significance of the death-to-life principle in the philosophy of Jesus. When Jesus made the prediction of his approaching death in the regions of Caesarea Philippi, he added that on the third day he would be raised up. In Mark 9:30-32 (Matthew 17:22f., Luke 9:43-45), the prophecy of his death is repeated, but again there is the promise, "he shall rise the third day." Yet again, in Mark 10:32-34 (Matthew 20:17-19, Luke 18:31-34) the prediction is repeated; but there follow the words, "and the third day he shall rise again." Thus Jesus saw his resurrection beyond the cross; his living again he knew to be the inevitable corollary of his death. Jesus would go to his cross, but he would go in full confidence that God would break the bonds of death for him and that he would walk triumphant from the grave. Obedience to death would bring liberation to life. In like manner Jesus saw that obedience to death would bring liberation to life for all who would take up a cross and follow him. He visualized for every disciple the *resurrection life* beyond a disciple's cross.

Now this resurrection life is none other than the life of victory over sin. Jesus recognized the sinfulnss of humanity. He saw every man in his unregenerate state as in bondage to sin. He saw the sin-death principle at work making slaves of men, and he knew there was but one remedy: the introduction of a higher principle into human experience that would liberate men from the operation of the sin-death principle. This principle he introduced into human experience when he died on his cross. Atonement was the practical result. His death, followed by his resurrection, was not merely a demonstration of what men might themselves achieve—it was itself the power given to men to achieve the victory over sin and death. Calvary was atonement and redemption which man could not provide for himself; the resurrection was the power of God given to humanity to rise from sin and death and find life eternal. The cross of the believer is the bending of the believer's will to the will of God, the tearing down of the walls of his ego that Christ's work on Calvary and his resurrection from the grave may become the power for the believer's rising from the grave of sin and self. Thus, as there was for Jesus an open grave beyond Calvary, for the believer there is beyond his cross new and abundant life. Paul states the matter thus:

> Therefore we are buried with him by baptism into death: that like as Christ was raised up from the dead by the glory of the Father, even so we also should walk in newness of life. For if we have been planted together in the likeness of his death, we shall be also in the likeness of his resurrection: knowing this, that our old man is crucified with him, that the body of sin might be destroyed, that henceforth we should not serve sin. For he that is dead is freed from sin. Now if we be dead with Christ, we believe that we shall also live with him: knowing that Christ being raised from the dead dieth no more; death hath no more dominion over him. For in that

he died, he died unto sin once: but in that he liveth, he liveth unto God. Likewise reckon ye also yourselves to be dead indeed unto sin, but alive unto God through Jesus Christ our Lord (Romans 6:4-11).

Men in sin are men in bondage; men who die with Christ are free men. They are free because they are right with God, but they are also free because the energies and endowments of their personalities are no longer dissipated in the trivialities and superficialities which sin imposes upon them, but are harnessed to the will of God. This means that these energies and endowments are directed toward self-realization and maximum personality development. The individual who takes up his cross to follow Jesus therefore wins the first victory that must be won in the search for his best self, the victory over sin.

We pass now to another aspect of the finding of one's life by taking up a cross to follow Jesus. This has to do with the achieving of goodness and holiness of character. We have seen that it is necessary to take up a cross and follow Jesus if one is to accept Jesus as his teacher and become a true disciple. The teachings of Jesus constitute a great body of principles of living. They are to be accepted and translated into living if what we call the way of Jesus is to be a way of life. One who takes up his cross and follows Jesus embraces these principles and endeavors with his best energy to translate them into daily living. Psychology teaches us that a man's habits become a part of the man himself, that what we practice that we become. The ethical system of Jesus is acknowledged, even by great non-Christian thinkers, to have no superior among all the ethical systems of the world. There is no goodness superior to the goodness which Jesus teaches. Men who make the earnest effort to practice without reservation the teachings of Jesus are recognized as good men, men of power, men of superior character and virtue. These are the men who accept the hard teachings of Jesus—those teachings that enjoin love of enemies, unlimited forgiveness, love of one's neighbor as oneself, turning the other cheek, recognition of the infinite worth of every human being without regard to race or station in life. Men who accept the entire ethical system of Jesus, including these hard teachings, are men who have taken up a cross to follow Jesus. They are good men, men of power, men of virtue, because by their practice of what Jesus teaches they have formed the character that is in keeping with the habits of life. The habit of practicing the ethical principles of Jesus produces the Jesus character. Thus does acceptance of the teachings of Jesus compel a man to be his best self; he can strive to be no less than his best self if he practices the teachings of Jesus; he must seek to be his best self to practice them. Not only does the practice of these principles call forth one's best energy, not only does obedience to them test one's faith and thereby strengthen faith, but they serve as a constant guide to that which is best in life in every situation. The person, therefore, who takes up his cross to follow Jesus need never be at a loss to know what is right and good in a given situation—his infallible guide is always near at hand; the standard of Jesus is that which prevents him from stumbling and leads him always to strive to be his best self in every situation. Again, therefore, we see the individual who goes with Jesus to a cross rising from his grave of self to find himself.

But to arise in newness of life with Christ is more than obedience to the teachings of Jesus, *it is to arise in fellowship with the living Christ.* Jesus is more than the Man of Galilee, and his way of life is more than his ethical system. Jesus arose from the grave, he lives, he is the Christ of eternal spirit! He lives in those who crucify self to follow him. Paul knew Christ, and Paul said, "I am crucified with Christ; no longer I live, but Christ lives in me." What Paul meant was that Christ had become incarnate in him. Now herein is the power for translating the teachings of Jesus into everyday living. Mortal man is too frail to obey Jesus in all things unless there is this power of the risen, living, indwelling Christ to provide the strength for obedience. Men who take up their crosses to follow Jesus know that Jesus is more than the Great Teacher; they find that he is a Person, a Presence, a Power, and they discover themselves in fellowship with him. He comes to them and lives in them because they open the doors of their souls to him; by the crucifixion of their own wills and the slaying of their pride, by thus confessing their own helplessness and need of him they unlock these doors. The indwelling Christ is a power, a power that releases the latent energies of personality, a power that shapes the personality in the likeness of the character of Christ himself. In truth, then, he who takes up his cross to follow Jesus finds his best possible self *because Christ finds him and lives in him, and does for him what he could never do for himself.* Surely it must be said of him in whom Christ lives that he has found his life.

An individual does not find his life apart from others. Jesus intended that a man should find his life among his fellows. The taking up of one's cross to follow Jesus sets a man in that relationship with others best designed to enable him to find his life. The way of the cross is not only the way of reconciliation with God, *it is the way of reconciliation between men.* Men are reconciled to one another when the walls between them are destroyed. These walls are erected by pride and egotism; he who takes up a cross to follow Jesus tears them down. Just as he crucifies self to allow Christ to enter his life, so he crucifies self to establish a relationship of trust, of exchange, of mutuality between himself and his fellow man. The taking up of a cross serves therefore to create for the individual a social climate which ministers to the growth of his own soul. Others become for him an object of loving consideration and service, he gladly gives to all and for the good of all. This calls forth from the individual those attitudes and actions that drive out fear, suspicion, contempt, and hatred of others, and that create within him the characteristics of the man of sympathy, kindness, and love. Giving is gaining and growing. The man who takes up his cross to follow Jesus gains and grows because he finds his highest joy in serving his fellows. He becomes a truly great man because he obeys Jesus' law of greatness: "Whosoever will be great among you, let him be your minister; And whosoever will be chief among you, let him be your servant" (Matthew 20:26-27). But not only does the individual who takes up his cross to follow Jesus gain and grow by giving, he grows also by *receiving*; for, having torn down the walls of self, he makes it possible for others to cross over the line between himself and his fellows. Those who cross that line do not come emptyhanded, they bring the treasures of their personalities and their experience with them. Jesus said to his disciples, "Blessed are the meek: for they shall inherit the earth." One of the choicest inheritances of earth are the gifts that come to us from the lives and personalities of others. Others become our friends, our neighbors, our helpers, our benefactors in a very real sense when we break down the walls of pride and selfishness that keep them from us. All men we know may become co-laborers with us in growing our souls, in building our personalities, in finding our best selves, if we are men who bear a cross. All this applies to the relationships which a man may establish with all his fellows. Jesus intended that we should hate none and love all, but there is a unique relationship that is established only between those who bear the cross; it is this relationship that is designed above all others to provide the climate *par excellence* of the Christian's growth. There is a family of God on earth, there is a beloved society: it is the assembly founded by the Christ, the *ekklēsia,* the *church.* It is in this society of the subjects of the Kingdom of God that the believer finds that mutuality and fellowship which contribute most of all the social influences necessary to his personality development. Among men, who, like himself, have taken up a cross to follow Jesus, he finds that sympathy, understanding, and support that are so necessary to completeness of life. In this society of cross-bearers he finds men with ideals and purposes akin to his own, men who have had an experience with God and with Christ similar to his own, men who have a like faith, men who will join with him in prayer to God the Father and service of the Lord Jesus Christ. In this group he will find men who will love him and support him when others fail him. In this fellowship he joins efforts with men whose hearts are fired by devotion to the cause he loves, men who are willing with him to die for that cause. This is a fellowship pervaded by radiance and joy, for it is composed of men and women who have discovered the secret of victorious living. In this fellowship the individual not only finds support and encouragement, but he also finds a place where he may sit at the feet of Jesus the Teacher, for the people of this fellowship endeavor to learn the way of Jesus and teach it to their fellows.

And so in the fellowship of those who bear the cross and follow Jesus the individual is given every incentive to be his best self and every encouragement to find his life. In the beloved society he likewise experiences the power of the Holy Spirit, witnesses him in action, and, like the men of Pentecost, is moved to give his witness of the things he has seen and heard. And so it is that a man loses his life to find it, but to find it in the midst of his fellows.

VI

JERUSALEM

Jesus approaches Jerusalem fully aware that he marches straight into the face of an evil storm. The sinister forces that go into the making of this storm have been gathering momentum against him almost from the beginning of his ministry. He has seen them from the first, seen them in the envy and hatred of the religious leaders, in the jealous concern of these leaders for the preservation of the system to which they owed their security. Jesus has determined that there is for him no escape from the storm. It is the will of God, it is his destiny, that he go to Jerusalem. He knows full well the fate that awaits him there. He knows this because he is no blind fanatic, as some have pictured him; he knows it because he is no wild apocalyptic dreamer, as others have portrayed him; he knows his fate because he is familiar with the laws of the spiritual cosmos and their working, because he is acquainted with sin, human nature and the laws of the mind, because he is capable of visualizing what happens when perfect love meets head-on with sin. As he approaches Jerusalem Jesus is no religious enthusiast courting a martyr's crown, he is a realist in full possession of his faculties, with but one aim: to accomplish the will of God. He comes to Jerusalem in complete mastery of himself and with his hands upon the controls of the events that are to focus about himself in the last week of his life. He will not be caught in this storm when it breaks over him like a frightened, helpless creature seized by a howling wind and dashed against the rocks. He will meet it and ride it out in the power of the Son of God. When the storm envelops him and brings him to the lowly portal of suffering and death, he is powerful in the strength of immortal love, and in most tragic defeat is most gloriously triumphant.

This storm at Jerusalem provides the supreme test of all that Jesus is or claims to be. Caught in the relentless force of this cataclysm, the character of Jesus will be revealed in stark nakedness. What he is will truly show itself. His conviction concerning himself and his mission, the consciousness of his uniqueness, his faith, his declarations concerning his Kingdom, his promises of reward—all these will be put to the severest test in this climactic week. Their genuineness or spuriousness will surely be known against the backdrop of the epochal events of this last visit to Jerusalem.

The consciousness of Jesus will be laid bare in this final week. We shall wish to see if what is therein revealed is in keeping with all that has been made known hitherto with respect to his conviction concerning himself. Shall we discover there the same underlying *motif* as to his death revealed on former occasions? Will he conduct himself when this climax comes as the Suffering Servant and maintain that consistency of character he has shown all along?

The quest for the mind of Jesus concerning himself will be conditioned in this final week by two new factors. The first of these is that he is no longer under restraint of silence concerning his Messiahship. He approaches Jerusalem for this final visit with the deliberate intent of publicly announcing his Messiahship. This public and official declaration of his Messiahship he conceives to be his inescapable duty. It is one of the chief reasons for his determination to proceed to Jerusalem in the face of certain death at the hands of the authorities. It is the divine imperative that he officially declare himself as the Messiah of the Jewish nation. We shall wish to observe with great care the conduct of Jesus and the deliberate portrayals he makes of his person within the context of this new situation, which calls for publication rather than secrecy concerning himself.

The other factor which introduces a new conditioning element into the quest for the mind of Jesus concerning himself is that he passes for the first time under control of other men. With his arrest he ceases to be a free agent, humanly speaking, and is subject to the coercion of others. Heretofore he has acted freely and only under limitations determined by his own will. It has been possible for him to precipitate, shape, and control events, but once he voluntarily surrenders himself to the Jerusalem authorities he is no longer the master of events, though he may exercise mastery of himself. Under such circumstances his conduct should prove revelatory in a new way of his mind and character. As he moves within this narrow context of coercion his words and acts will reveal his inconsistency, if there be any such in him, or they will show in bold relief the sublime integrity and moral grandeur of his person.

These factors need to be kept in mind, therefore, as we search for the revelations of the mind of Jesus which this climactic week affords.

I. The Royal Entry

(Mark 11:1-11; Matthew 21:1-11; Luke 19:29-44)

The primary source of the narrative of the so-called "triumphal entry" is Mark. Significant additions, of which due notice will be taken, are made by both Matthew and Luke.

The royal entry is highly important in the quest for the mind of Jesus because it was deliberately planned by him as the method by which he would publicly and officially declare himself as the Messiah of the Jewish nation. When this careful planning is understood, the significance of the event in revealing the messianic self-consciousness of Jesus is immediately apparent. If we can see in this act a deliberate self-revelation of Jesus we can claim for it the highest value as evidence in the search for his thinking concerning himself in these climactic days of the final week. It will be possible to compare this evidence with the conclusions heretofore drawn as to his messianic consciousness and to determine whether or not the Jesus who rides into Jerusalem upon an ass is the same Jesus who emerged from the wilderness of Judea victorious over Satan.

The evidence is clear that Jesus made careful preparation

for the royal entry. The manner of the securing of the animal upon which he rode into the city shows that he had made arrangements in advance for its use. The Synoptics agree on the details revealing the pre-arrangement, except that Matthew mentions two animals instead of one. This presents no difficulty, since the animal upon which Jesus rode was one that had never been ridden before; that is, a colt—a fact which would explain the presence of its mother. According to the Synoptic narrative, two of the disciples of Jesus were to go "into the village over against you" where they were to find "a colt tied, whereon never man sat." Matthew at this point mentions the colt and its mother. The instruction of Jesus to the disciples, according to Mark, was, "loose him, and bring him." The disciples were further instructed by Jesus concerning the answer they were to give if they were accosted by anyone and asked why they were loosing the colt. They were to answer, according to Mark and Luke, "The Lord hath need of him," or, as Matthew has it, "the Lord hath need of them." Mark and Luke go on to describe how the colt was secured in precisely the manner in which Jesus said he would be secured, while Matthew contents himself with the bare statement of the fact that "the disciples went, and did as Jesus commanded them, and brought the ass and the colt."

Closer scrutiny of the saying, "the Lord hath need of him," will show that a mistranslation of the Greek is largely responsible for the common misunderstanding of this incident. In the Greek the sentence is *Ho kurios autou chreian echei.* Matthew gives the saying in precisely the same way, except for the singular form *autou* the plural form *autōn* occurs. The position of the pronoun *autou* suggests, and almost demands, a much more natural rendition of the saying, namely, *"the Lord of him has need,"* or, if we take Matthew's account, *"the Lord of them has need."* This immediately suggests that Jesus was the owner of the animal and prior to this had either bought it or secured it as a gift. This interpretation of the saying is strongly corroboratetd by the fact that the word *kurios* means "owner," as well as "lord" or "master." It was the anxiety of the translators to apply the term to Jesus as *Lord* that obscured the fact that the meaning here is *owner*. What the disciples were to say to their questioners was in fact, therefore, "the owner of him [or, of them] has need." This saying was a "password" given by Jesus to the two disciples as a means of securing the animal from the former owners at the appointed time. It was obviously a "password" that had been agreed on in advance by Jesus and the former owners of the colt.

It is possible to recognize important implications in the use of this "password" by Jesus to secure the animal for the royal entry. First of all, it suggests great care and deliberate planning on his part for the entry into Jerusalem. Having taken the trouble to buy or secure as a gift in advance this animal for the specific purpose of using it for the entry into the city, he assuredly viewed this entry and the manner of its execution as of great importance. It was the result of his deliberate choice and planning that the animal was an ass, and further that it was a colt that had never before carried a rider. By his choice of the animal Jesus designed that truths of great importance should be revealed in the manner of his entry into the city. He intended that the ass would suggest the nature of his Messiahship, and that the fact of its being a colt never before ridden would suggest the uniqueness of this momentous event.

It is also possible to see in this pre-arranged password a suggestion of the secrecy with which Jesus was compelled to surround his plans for the entry into Jerusalem. It was not possible for him to share the knowledge of these plans with his own disciples. This was due in part to the imminent treachery of Judas, and in part to the danger that other members of the twelve, as well as Judas, would upset his plans for the official presentation of himself as Messiah to the nation. Jesus had determined the time and the manner of this presentation; he determined that these should accord with certain prophetic patterns to which he had committed himself; revelation of the plans, even to the disciples, would endanger their execution, hence he was forced to the adoption of secrecy in their formulation and execution. In so far as Judas was concerned there was the danger that he would deliver Jesus to the authorities before it would be possible for him to make the official presentation of himself to the nation as Messiah; in so far as the remainder of the twelve were concerned, there was the possibility that they would encourage a premature acclamation of Jesus as Messiah by the multitudes. In such a premature acclamation Jesus could foresee the prevention of much teaching and activity that he deemed necessary to the fulfilment of his ministry in the final week. It is quite likely that another reason was responsible for the secrecy with which Jesus surrounded his plans, namely, a wish that the demonstration of the multitudes, when it came, should be spontaneous and in no sense the work of the twelve. If this was his wish it was fulfilled.

The day was the first day of Passover Week (Sunday) and only four days prior to the day on which the Passover lamb was slain (the 14th of Nisan, Thursday). The city was crowded with pilgrims come for the celebration of the greatest of all the feasts. Along the road that Jesus came from Bethany was a constant stream of pilgrims. They were aware of Jesus' nearness to them. Word had gone ahead into the city of his approach. There was therefore in existence an atmosphere of expectancy and curiosity with reference to this visit of Jesus, especially among the Galileans, among whom he was well known. The news of his preparations to ride an ass into the city would travel through the crowds with great rapidity. The easily aroused Galileans would be quick to attach significance to these preparations. The magnitude and spontaneity of the demonstration aroused by his approach to the city are not difficult to understand in the light of the great popularity which Jesus had won in Galilee and the effort made by the Galileans on the occasion of the feeding of the five thousand to take him by force and make him king.

Jesus, contrary to the attitude he had taken heretofore with reference to demonstrations in his behalf, accepted the enthusiastic adulation and acclamation of the throngs. After the feeding of the five thousand in Galilee he had compelled the disciples to leave the scene and summarily dismissed the multitudes when the effort was made to compel him to accept the crown (Mark 6:45-46; John 6:15); on other occasions he sought to escape from the crowds, but now he gladly accepts the approving shouts of the throngs. The conduct and words of the shouting people show plainly that they understand the act of Jesus to be a declaration on his part that he is the Messiah. They spread their garments in the roadway before him, thus exhibiting deference due only to a king. They wave palm branches and shout: "Hosanna to the Son of David: Blessed is he that cometh in the name of the Lord; Hosanna in the highest" (Matthew 21:9). These people from Galilee are delirious with joy that he has at last consented to declare himself as Messiah. They show their understanding of his claims by acclaiming him as the son of David. And Jesus accepts the demonstration. Is he willing now to take the crown? When the sullen Pharisees from Jerusalem demand that he rebuke the multitudes he refuses the request and declares, "I tell you that, if these should hold their peace, the stones would immediately cry out" (Luke 19:40).

What is in the mind of Jesus as he deliberately precipitates this wild demonstration in his behalf and gratefully accepts the acclamation of himself by the multitudes as the son of David? Is it indeed that he has in mind the acceptance of the crown which he refused in Galilee? Is he acting in a manner that is inconsistent with the decisions he made in the wilderness, the declaration he made at Nazareth, the reply he sent to John the Baptist, the revelation he made at Caesarea Philippi? Is it that he hopes this great demonstration will by its magnitude overwhelm the religious authorities and compel them to accept him and give to him the throne of David? And when this does not result from the demonstration, is it not true that his voluntary surrender to the authorities becomes an act of disappointment, grief, and martrydom? So it might be argued by those who will not take the pains to study with care the gospel records.

In the midst of this his greatest hour of triumph Jesus entertained no illusions concerning the fate that awaited him; he expected no miracle to transform the hardened hearts of the men who held the destiny of the nation in their hands. Luke records the melancholy story of what transpired when Jerusalem came into view as Jesus and the cheering throngs approached the city from the Mount of Olives. He broke into weeping (*eklausen*—ingressive Aorist) and cried out, "If thou hadst known, even thou, at least in this thy day, the things which belong unto peace! but now they are hid from thine eyes." Jesus then predicts the coming destruction of the city, giving as the reason for its fate, "because thou knewest not the time of thy visitation" (19:41-44). No, if we are to believe Luke's narrative here, and there is no cause to doubt it, Jesus did not precipitate this demonstration in order to compel the Jerusalem authorities to give him the crown which the multitudes had pressed upon him in Galilee.

No, Jesus had not forsaken the spiritual pattern of Messiahship to which he committed himself in the wilderness of Judea. His conduct was never more indicative of his fidelity to the prophetic and spiritual pattern, for see him in this his hour of greatest triumph, in this hour when he makes official presentation of himself to the nation as its Messiah, in this hour when the glad shouts of the people echo in his ears as they acclaim him the son of David—behold him approaching his capital to claim his throne, riding upon an ass! The sorry picture he makes as the little animal slowly bears him along the rocky road, his feet almost dragging the dust, is in ridiculous contrast to the majestic acclamations of the multitudes. The blindness of the people to this contrast can only be explained by the great elevation of their spirits generated by their common admiration for Jesus and by their ardent hope for the coming of the Kingdom. In their enthusiasm for the enthronement of Jesus as David's son they have lost sight of the lesson of the ass. But there he rides upon an ass that he himself has chosen with the deliberate intent of using him to reveal the character of Israel's true Messiah as he comes to Jerusalem to claim David's throne! In later years, as Matthew compiled his Gospel, he read aright the mind of Jesus on this occasion when he declared: "All this was done, that it might be fulfilled which was spoken by the prophet, saying, Tell ye the daughter of Zion, Behold, thy King cometh unto thee, meek, and sitting upon an ass, and a colt the foal of an ass" (21:4f.).

Is Jesus aware that the multitudes do not comprehend the true character of the Messiah whom they are so gladly acclaiming as the son of David? Undoubtedly he is. Then why does he not pause as he moves on to the city and declaim to the people that they are wrong? Why does he not rebuke them, as indeed the Pharisees wished him to do? There are several answers at hand. Jesus indicated one of these, perhaps the chief one, in his reply to the Pharisees: "If these should hold their peace, the stones would immediately cry out." By this Jesus indicated, first, the impossibility of quenching the enthusiasm of the crowds, and, second, his belief in the predestined necessity of this acclamation. With further reference to the latter point, Jesus believed that it was a necessity inherent in the unfolding of the historical events of which he was in that hour the center that he should be acclaimed the son of David. The acclamation was appropriate to this highly important historical situation and cannot be disturbed without violence to history. The people would have listened to no didactic discourse from Jesus correcting their false notions in that hour of mass enthusiasm. Jesus was content to let the unforgettable picture of himself riding upon an ass to claim his throne be the historical answer to the erroneous conceptions of his Messiahship entertained by the people. Again, we may believe that he was unwilling to interrupt the demonstration to correct the false notions of the people because he was conscious of the value of the glad, spontaneous acclamation of himself as Messiah for fulfilling the prophetic pattern he now followed and for the completion of a valid historical record for the benefit of posterity.

The very prophecy of Zechariah (9:9) quoted here by Matthew in explanation of the manner of Jesus' entry was undoubtedly the prophetic pattern he chose for the official presentation of himself as Messiah to the nation. In order to see the pattern in greater detail, it is necessary to go beyond the quotation and understand the context from which it is taken. Having predicted the destruction of the heathen cities round about, the prophet turns his attention to Jerusalem and declares:

> Rejoice greatly, O daughter of Zion; shout, O daughter of Jerusalem: behold, thy King cometh unto thee: he is just, and having salvation; lowly, and riding upon an ass, and upon a colt the foal of an ass. And I will cut off the chariot from Ephraim, and the horse from Jerusalem, and the battle bow shall be cut off: and he shall speak peace unto the heathen: and his dominion shall be from sea even to sea, and from the river even to the ends of the earth (Zechariah 9: 9-10).

The prophet visualizes the coming of a king to Jerusalem who will conquer and rule by justice rather than by force. This king will come in peace, riding upon an ass, and the promise is that Jehovah will "cut off the chariot from Ephraim, and the horse from Jerusalem, and the battle bow shall be cut off." Horse, chariot, and bow are the symbols of battle, but these instruments of warfare, according to the prophet, will not be utilized by Jehovah in establishing the new kingdom of righteousness, a universal kingdom, which will stretch "from sea even to sea, and from the river even to the ends of the earth." The king who will reign over this Kingdom will renounce the instruments of force and warfare—"he is just, and having salvation." His character as a king of peace will be shown in the manner of his approach to Jerusalem; he will come not in a chariot of war, not upon a battle steed, but "lowly, and riding upon an ass."

Jesus conceived himself to be this king of righteousness and peace as he offered himself to the Jewish nation as its sovereign. This was the prophetic pattern to which he committed himself as he claimed the throne of David. His lament over the city fully corroborates this interpretation of his act in approaching Jerusalem riding upon an ass. His lament was: "If thou hadst known, even thou, at least in this thy day, *the things which belong unto peace!*" (Luke 19:42.) He saw clearly the folly of the Jewish dream of emancipation by force of arms. In his lament he foresaw the inevitable doom of the city because of its blind insistence upon force in the effort to establish its independence. "For the days shall come upon thee," he said, "that thine enemies shall cast a trench about thee, and compass thee round, and keep thee in on every side, And shall lay thee even with the ground, and thy children within thee; and they shall not leave in thee one stone upon another; because thou knewest not the time of thy visitation" (Luke 19:43 f.).

In offering himself to the Jewish nation as the King of Peace, Jesus was pointing his people to their only way of salvation. His plan was realistic and practical. Its acceptance by the Jews would have averted the great calamity which befell the nation in A.D. 70 when the Romans captured the city and destroyed the Temple. The blind refusal of the Jews to accept Jesus as the Messiah brought untold woes upon them, just as the refusal of Jews and Gentiles alike to accept him as the King of Peace has continued to bring upon humanity the evils and horrors of war. The Romans were not harsh overlords when subject peoples co-operated with them. The way which Jesus proposed to his people was the way of love; it demanded of the Jews that they surrender their narrow and fanatical nationalism and co-operate with the Romans in the establishment of peace and order. It called for the renunciation of force in their dealings with their conquerors. But beyond these requirements was the greater demand that the Jews should recognize the universal mission of Israel and accept the implications of all Jehovah's past dealings with his Chosen People. The nation stood at the parting of the ways, stood at its last great hour of destiny, when Jesus came riding into the city upon the lowly ass. Jesus was presenting to Israel its final opportunity to fulfil its historic mission to the world and become in truth the "conqueror" of the world. The day of the nation's "visitation" had come, the hour of destiny had struck. Jerusalem might now become indeed the "capital" of the great universal Kingdom of Righteousness. It was spiritual blindness, pride, narrow nationalism, and devotion to legalism in religion that prevented the leaders of the nation from recognizing Jesus as the Messiah and accepting his way as the way of salvation. The leaders were not prepared to accept the revolutionary demands of Jesus for a spiritual rebirth of Israel. It is true that if the Jewish nation had accepted Jesus as Messiah, the nation would have ceased to exist in the old narrow nationalistic sense, but having lost itself as the Israel of old it would have found itself in the new universal Israel of the Kingdom of God.

And so Jesus rode on to Jerusalem upon the lowly ass, knowing full well that he was the true son of David and Israel's rightful King. He might have come in different guise, upon a horse or in chariot, and then the leaders would have welcomed him, but he could not come thus because even as he approached his capital as King he was the Servant of Jehovah, the King who was prepared to suffer and die for his ideal and for his people.

The Jesus who rode upon the lowly ass to Jeursalem was the same Jesus who came out of the wilderness of Judea victorious over Satan.

II. The Cleansing of the Temple

(Mark 11:15-18; Matthew 21:12-16; Luke 19:45-48)

The Markan source is the primary source here.

It is significant that Jesus follows up the royal entry in which he officially presented himself to the nation as Messiah by this remarkable demonstration in the Temple. There is no question but that the cleansing of the Temple was designed by Jesus as a manifestation of his messianic authority. It was by no means the result of a sudden outburst of indignation or anger. Jesus had been fully aware all along of the trade in animals and the business of money-changing carried on in the Temple courts with the approval of the priests. It could not have been a surprise to him when on the day after the royal entry he arrived at the Temple and saw the traders and the money-changers at work. There was the expression of righteous indignation in the act but certainly not of uncontrolled anger.

The cleansing of the Temple was a part of the public and official avowal by Jesus of himself as Messiah. In the act he gave demonstration of his authority as the Messiah.

The Temple would be the normal scene for a great manifestation of the Messiah—such would be the belief of the religious leaders and the people. The prophecy of Malachi was: "the Lord, whom ye seek, shall suddenly come to his temple" (3:1). The Temple, as the heart of the religious life of the nation, would most naturally be conceived of as the seat of the Messiah's throne and power. This sentiment was responsible in part, as we saw, for the temptation that came to Jesus in the wilderness to cast himself down from the Temple. In refusing this suggestion of Satan, Jesus renounced the Temple and the Temple system as necessary to his messianic work. He adhered to this decision throughout his ministry, for although he used the Temple courts for purposes of teaching, he never at any time allied himself with the priests or the Levitical system. At the same time he recognized the Temple and the Levitical system as occupying places of importance in the historical purposes of God, and he observed with a sense of sorrow and indignation the prostitution of the Temple and the Levitical system by the ruling priests to purposes of material gain. He knew that the sale of animals for sacrifice and the business of exchanging the Temple tax coins for Roman money had become a source of great revenue to the priests, who had become rich by controlling the concessions by which the trading and money-changing in the Temple courts were made possible. In this prostitution of the Temple and the Levitical system to purposes of money-making Jesus saw a gross violation of the purposes of these great institutions. In the exhibition of himself as the Messiah Jesus asserted his rightful authority over the Temple in this act of purging it from the taint of commercialism. Surely he realized that by one manifestation of indignation he could not effect the permanent cleansing that was needed; his purpose was to demonstrate his messianic authority by performing an act that asserted his right to control the life and activity of the Temple. Mark brings out this point graphically when he says, Jesus "would not suffer that any man should carry a vessel through the Temple" (11:16).

How different is this manifestation of messianic power in the Temple from that which Satan suggested Jesus should make! Satan would have had Jesus resort to a demonstration of supernatural power by flinging himself from a high point of the structure in defiance of natural law. When Jesus comes to the Temple to manifest his messianic authority, however, he limits himself to the exercise of moral and spiritual power. This manifestation is magnificent and awesome, because it is altogether a demonstration of spiritual power. Once again we witness the fidelity of Jesus to his previously chosen patterns, once more we see his integrity, once again we see in him the fusion of majesty and lowliness, the combination of the splendor of the Son of God and Son of Man with the meekness of the Servant of Jehovah. Only as the Servant of Jehovah could Jesus have clothed himself with the restraint shown by him as he manifested himself as the Messiah with authority over the Temple. Jesus is acting precisely as the character which was revealed by him in the wilderness of Judea and in the synagogue at Nazareth determined that he would act when he came to Jerusalem to proclaim himself as the Messiah in the Temple of God.

There are those who, failing to understand this act of Jesus, charge that he resorted to the use of physical force in ejecting the traders from the Temple. If this is true, he violated the decisions he made in the wilderness and acted in a manner contrary to the previous revelations which he had made of his character. In the wilderness of Judea he renounced the use of physical force in the achievement of his objectives, and while the physical ejection of traders from the Temple courts would constitute a limited use of force, it would be the use of physical force, nevertheless, and in this it would be part and parcel of the acceptance of the use of physical force as a principle. If Jesus ejected the traders by physical means, he was not acting as the Servant of Jehovah; and if he is not now the Servant of Jehovah as he comes to Jerusalem to face the employment of physical violence against himself, he is inconsistent with all that he has revealed of his mind and character up to now.

In their eagerness to use this incident to justify war and the use of physical violence, men have too often done injustice to the character of Jesus. The view of Jesus concerning war is not involved here, but the integrity of his character is. It is quite clear that *Jesus renounced the use of violence in any form as a method of establishing his authority or propagating his gospel.* With this agrees his specific command to Peter to put up the sword when Peter attempted to defend him in the garden of Gethsemane (Matthew 26:52; John 18:11). In the narratives of the cleansing of the Temple there is no statement that Jesus touched the traders. It is said that he overthrew the tables of the money-changers, and the seats of the sellers of doves, but there is no suggestion that he laid hands on the money-changers and the traders. It was the majesty of his person and the spiritual power that was manifest in his face and his words that awed these traders and compelled them to arise from their places of business and scurry from the Temple courts. His overturning of the money tables and the seats of the dove-sellers was part of the symbolism of the entire act of cleansing the Temple. It was moral and spiritual power, manifested on a magnificent scale, not physical violence, that enabled Jesus to accomplish his purpose. The very first manifestation of physical violence on his part would have broken the spell of spiritual power, and in an instant the outraged traders would have rushed upon him and torn him to pieces. By limiting himself to the exhibition of spiritual power Jesus was not only true to himself as the Servant of Jehovah, he was able also to demonstrate his authority over the Temple as the true Messiah of Israel.

III. The Conflict with the Religious Leaders

The conduct of Jesus, particularly in the cleansing of the Temple, brings him into inevitable conflict with the religious leaders. He makes no effort to escape from them but meets them face to face. It is not appropriate to our purpose to consider all that transpired in these instances of public conflict. Our interest is centered in what the conflict reveals as to consciousness of Jesus concerning his person and mission. What is in his mind about himself as he meets the religious leaders face to face? What does he reveal to them concerning himself? Does he yield under the pressure of these men to opportunism? Is his attitude and method of approach to them in keeping with his character as the Servant of Jehovah? When at last the storm he has seen from afar begins to beat in his face, what conviction does Jesus have concerning himself and his mission? These are the questions we shall endeavor to find answer to in those conversations of Jesus with the religious leaders. It is only necessary to consider two of the great parables used by Jesus in these conversations, and the discussion incident to the question as to whose son the Messiah was, to find the answers to our questions. The parables that must be considered are the parable of the wicked husbandmen and the parable of the marriage feast of the king's son. Mark is the primary source of the former, while Matthew alone gives the latter, indicating that the parable is from his special source *M*.

1. *The parable of the wicked husbandmen.* Mark 12:1-12; Matthew 21:33-46; Luke 20:9-19. This parable was addressed to the religious leaders. They are enumerated in Mark and Luke as the "chief priests," the "scribes," and the "elders" (Mark 11:27; Luke 20:1). Matthew mentions the "chief priests" and the "elders" but omits mention of the "scribes" (21:23). The Gospel writers wish to make it clear that Jesus is now face to face with the rulers of the nation. They had found him in the Temple and challenged his authority (Mark 11:28), but Jesus had baffled them by asking them to tell him whether the baptism of John was from heaven or from men. When they indicated their unwillingness to commit themselves on this question, Jesus refused to answer their demand that he reveal the source of his authority. His reason for the refusal was that their inability to recognize the authority of John the Baptist disqualified them as judges of Jesus' authority. According to Matthew, Jesus then told the parable of the two sons, the one who refused to work in his father's vineyard but afterward repented, the other who stubbornly refused to go into the vineyard—the purpose of the parable being to show how the "publicans and harlots"

went into the Kingdom while the religious leaders failed to enter. The parable of the wicked husbandmen follows.

The parable is of a man who planted a vineyard and let it out to husbandmen as he took his journey into another country. When the owner later sent a servant to receive the owner's share of the fruit, the husbandmen beat him and sent him away empty. Another servant was sent with similar results. A third servant was killed by the wicked husbandmen; others were sent with the result that some were beaten and some were killed. At last the owner of the vineyard sent his beloved son to collect his rightful share of the fruits, in the hope that husbandmen would respect and receive him as the son of the master of the vineyard, but the wicked husbandmen reasoned that since he was the heir he should be put out of the way, so they killed him. In reply to Jesus' question, "What shall therefore the lord of the vineyard do?" the answer that Jesus himself gives, according to Mark, is: "he will come and destroy the husbandmen, and will give the vineyard unto others." Jesus then concludes this conversation with the question: "And have ye not read this scripture; The stone which the builders rejected is become the head of the corner: this was the Lord's doing, and it is marvelous in our eyes?"

This is a parable of judgment upon the Jewish nation. Its lesson is clear. Jesus sees himself as the beloved son in the parable who is sent last by the master of the vineyard and is killed by the wicked husbandmen. In this manner he portrays himself as being sent by God as the climax of a long series of historical approaches to the people of Israel. The vineyard is the nation's historic mission in the world; the husbandmen of course represent the leaders of the nation. The servants who came to the vineyard and were rejected one after another are the prophets from Moses to John the Baptist. The parable reveals with awful simplicity the persistent refusal of the nation's leadership to accept the unfailing efforts of Jehovah to win the people to the way of righteousness. Its chief interest for our purpose, however, is what it reveals concerning Jesus' estimate of his own place in this historical process having to do with God's dealing with Israel. The parable shows that Jesus conceived of his work as the great climax of this process. He sees himself as the beloved Son of the owner of the vineyard. This can be interpreted in no other way than a claim by Jesus of the unique relationship to God of Son. Those who came before the heir in the parable were servants. The last who came was *the heir* and *beloved son*. Since Jesus sees himself as the heir in the parable, it is suggestive of his conviction that he has a right to demand and expect of the nation the fruit that they owe to God, in other words the fulfilment of the nation's historic mission to the world. The exalted and unique position in which Jesus visualizes himself is further emphasized by the indication that in him God is making his *last and crowning effort to win the nation.* Beyond the refusal of the nation to accept him as Messiah he sees but one consequence: the destruction of the national leadership and the passing of Israel's stewardship to others. This can mean but one thing, the death of the theocracy and the end of the Jewish state. Beloved son, heir, God's last and climactic messenger at the apex of the long historical process of Jehovah's dealings with his people—in this fashion does Jesus see himself as he stands face to face with the men who hold the destiny of the nation in their hands. Finally he appeals to the messianic Psalm (118) in support of the lesson of the parable. The beloved son and heir is also the stone which the builders rejected and which was made the "head of the corner." According to an addition which Matthew makes to the narrative, Jesus interprets this allusion to the rejected stone in this manner: "Therefore say I unto you, the kingdom of God shall be taken from you, and given to a nation bringing forth the fruits thereof. And whosoever shall fall on this stone shall be broken: but on whomsoever it shall fall, it will grind him to powder."

This latter teaching is significant as revealing Jesus' consciousness of the universal character of his mission. He, the rejected stone, is to become the cornerstone of some building. What building? Certainly not old Israel, for Jesus was fully aware of the approaching doom of the Jewish state. The building is the new structure (the term being used only in a figurative sense, of course) of the universal Kingdom of God. Of this vast and indestructible edifice arising after his death, Jesus sees himself as the cornerstone. Also he is conscious of the vast importance of the position he will occupy in history, for this cornerstone, which he himself will be, will serve as the determinative factor in the destinies of men. He will stand forever as the unbreakable stone of history; men who reject him will but stumble over this stone to break themselves in pieces; men who seek to remove the stone from its rightful place of pre-eminence will find themselves crushed to dust beneath its awful weight.

It was thus that Jesus pronounced judgment upon the religious leaders for their rejection of him as the Messiah. Interwoven with the teaching is the revelation of a consciousness that he and his mission occupy absolutely unique places in history. It is very clear that Jesus sees himself in a position in history which none other before him occupied and no other after him will occupy. He is exalted and alone in that awesome place. At the same time he is conscious that his death is a part of the historical process that leads to this place of eminence. In all of this claim and prophecy of uniqueness and exaltation is the grim picture of the rejection and slaying of the beloved son and heir. But it is a matter of surpassing importance that in the mind of Jesus *the beloved son who was rejected and killed is also the stone which was to become the head of the corner.*

This synthesis of the ideas of rejection and exaltation, of death and glory is not new to Jesus. He recognized it and accepted it for himself when in the wilderness of Judea he saw that he was both Son of God and Servant of Jehovah! He re-affirmed it at Caesarea Philippi when he revealed that the Son of Man and the Christ the Son of the living God must go to Jerusalem and suffer rejection and death at the hands of the leaders of the nation.

2. *The parable of the marriage feast of the king's son.* Matthew 22:1-14. The teaching of this parable is quite similar to that of the parable of the wicked husbandmen. The rejection of Jesus as Messiah by the religious leaders of Israel is represented here in the refusal of invited guests

to attend the marriage feast which a king made for his son. God's judgment upon the leaders for the rejection of Messiah is portrayed in the act of the king in sending his armies to destroy the murderers of his servants. The presentation of the Kingdom to Israel is pictured as the marriage feast to which the leaders are invited; the offer of the Kingdom to others than the old Israel is seen in the invitation which was extended to uninvited guests from the "highways," people who were "both bad and good." The necessity that all who enter the Kingdom shall accept the demands of the Kingdom is a further lesson that is pressed home in the case of the guest who sat down to the feast without having put on a wedding garment and who was thrown into the "outer darkness" because of his failure to clothe himself appropriately for the feast.

In his reply to the question of the disciples of John the Baptist concerning fasting, Jesus had referred to himself as the "Bridegroom" (Mark 2:18f.). At that time he had said that the days would come when the Bridegroom would be taken away from the "sons of the bridechamber." Jesus is now in the midst of these days of the "taking away" of the Bridegroom. Apparently he has not forgotten his former reference to himself as the Bridegroom. In this parable he pictures himself as the king's Son whose approaching marriage occasions the great feast.

The significance of the parable for our present purpose is its suggestiveness of the conception which Jesus held with reference to his mission. In this particular the parable is confirmatory of the teaching of the parable of the wicked husbandmen. Again Jesus occupies the place of honor in the story. In the former parable he was the "beloved son" and "heir"; here he is the king's Son for whom a great marriage feast is made. The Son's exalted position is magnified in the great preparations made for the feast, in the king's insistence that the feast must be held in spite of the refusal of the invited guests to come, in the diligent effort to secure guests in the "highways," and in the insistence of the king that all shall recognize the importance of the occasion and honor the son by wearing a wedding garment.

In this parable Jesus sets forth clearly the supreme importance of his mission in the history of Israel. It was his "marriage" that occasioned the offer of the Kingdom of God to Israel, represented as the great marriage feast of the king's son. Jesus clearly indicates his conviction that his mission is universal and will not be thwarted by the rejection of the Kingdom by the leaders of the nation. This is shown by the calling of uninvited guests in the parable. Again we see in Jesus his awareness of his unique position in history and his consciousness of the historical and universal significance of his work. His parable reveals his conviction that he was the King's Son for whom there was one great marriage feast which was of epochal importance, both for those who were invited and refused to come and for those who were invited and came.

3. *The question concerning the Messiah as David's son.* Mark 12:35-37; Matthew 22:41-46; Luke 20:41-44. It was after the leaders had failed to trap him with the questions concerning the payment of tribute to Caesar, the woman who had seven husbands, and the greatest commandment, that Jesus propounded to them the question concerning the Messiah as the son of David. We shall examine this conversation with a view to discovering what it reveals as to the messianic consciousness of Jesus.

According to Mark the question of Jesus was: "How say the scribes that the Christ [*ho Cristos*—the Messiah] is the son of David?" Matthew's narrative is slightly different. His version is that Jesus asked the Pharisees: "What think ye of the Christ [*ton Christon*]? whose son is he?" Matthew represents the Pharisees as replying to Jesus' question, "of David." Matthew continues the narrative (Mark and Luke practically paralleling his report) by representing Jesus as saying: "How then doth David in spirit call him Lord, saying, The Lord said unto my Lord, Sit thou on my right hand, till I make thine enemies thy footstool? If David then call him Lord, how is he his son?" Matthew's succinct report of the effect of Jesus' question is: "And no man was able to answer him a word."

The failure of the Pharisees to reply to Jesus' question

is evidence that they agreed in part with his interpretation of this passage from the one hundred and tenth Psalm Their silence indicates that the scribes themselves interpreted this psalm as messianic and believed that David was the author and therefore the speaker. It likewise reflected the common view that the Messiah was to be the son of David. The critical question as to the authorship of the Psalm need not enter into this discussion. The critical view is that David is represented as the speaker.[1] It is apparent from the conversation under consideration that both Jesus and the scribes believed that David was the author and speaker. The conclusion remains the same whether the former or latter view as to authorship be adopted: David said that someone called by him "my Lord" was told by "the Lord" to sit at the Lord's right hand until the enemies of the person called by David "my Lord" were made his "footstool." The Hebrew makes it clear that it is Jehovah who speaks to David, the term translated "the Lord" being *Yahweh.* The person spoken of as "my Lord" by David is *adhoni.* Who was the person David could speak of as "my Lord?" The tenor of the Psalm as a whole justifies the view of Jesus and the scribes that this person was a "son" of David, that is, a future king of David's line. That David is thinking of the perpetuity of his line is indicated by the statement (verse 4): "The Lord [i.e., Jehovah] hath sworn, and will not repent, Thou [i.e., David] art a priest for ever after the order of Melchizedek." David visualizes the permanence of his throne, but he is conscious of present limitations as applicable both to himself as monarch and to his throne as an institution. He sees the fulfilment of Jehovah's promise that his throne will be established "for ever" in a "son," one of his line, whom he gladly speaks of as "my Lord." This one will be given the honor of sitting at Jehovah's right hand, the place of eminence and authority that a monarch would reserve for his son and heir. Thus David recognizes the fact that his "son" who will establish the Davidic throne forever must be more

---

[1] See The Psalms in *International Critical Commentary, ad loc.*

than David's son—he must be Jehovah's Son. This is why David can speak of him as "my Lord."

The religious leaders accept the fact that the Messiah must be David's son, but they are unable to tell, or they will not tell, why David speaks of him as "Lord." They are aware of Jesus' claim to be the son of David; they remember that only two days have passed since he refused to silence the multitudes when they acclaimed him as the son of David. Perhaps they recognize only too well the implications of his question and are afraid to commit themselves to a position that can be interpreted in any way as favorable to his claims. They fall back upon silence as the safe policy. Thus they fail, either because of ignorance or willfulness to accept the truth that David had grasped long before, namely, that the true Messiah must be more than the son of David—he must be also the Son of God.

But Jesus knew this, saw it clearly, and gladly accepted the prophetic pattern his "father" David had drawn. It is hardly debatable that Jesus reveals in this conversation his own messianic consciousness and his conviction that he is the person of whom David spoke when he said, "Jehovah said unto my Lord, sit thou at my right hand." He had presented himself to the nation in the royal entry two days prior to this as the son of David. Here, then, we can see the working of a *Q.E.D.* in his own mind as he raises this question with the Pharisees. Since he is the son of David he is the one to whom Jehovah saws, "Sit thou at my right hand"—he is Jehovah's Son, the Son of God. If the rulers had accepted him as David's son, they would then have been faced with the necessity of accepting him as the Son of God, had they followed the pattern of spiritual Messiahship implied in David's saying. Jesus saw himself as fulfilling the demands of this pattern long prior to this debate. He was conscious of his unique Sonship when he heard the voice from heaven at his baptism, and it was on the basis of this unique relationship as Son that he fought out his battle with Satan in the wilderness of Judea. To be the true Son of David is to be the Son of God, and to be the Son of God is to express that Sonship in the person of One who is actually, ideally, and spiritually the son of

David. As the Son of David he is the ideal King of Israel, the typical Israelite, the One who heads up in his person the historical stream of Jehovah's dealing with his Chosen People, the One in whom the promises of Jehovah to his people are validated. As the Son of God he is the universal Saviour and Redeemer, the great Son of Man in whom all history heads up, the perfect revealer of God to all mankind in all ages, the King of kings and Lord of lords.

But the leaders of Israel had their eyes upon a Messiah of a different sort. He was son of David, yes, but he was less than the Son David saw he must be. Because they could not see him as David saw him, and because they failed to see in Jesus this true Son of David and Son of God, they failed in the great hour of Israel's visitation. Jesus saw that it would be thus, but he faithfully gave to the nation the witness of that One he knew himself to be.

IV. The Last Passover and the Giving of the New Covenant

(Mark 14: 12-26; Matthew 26:17-30; Luke 22:7-38)

The primary source of the narrative of the celebration of the Passover and institution of the Lord's Supper by Jesus and the twelve is Mark, but it will be seen by comparison of the Synoptics here that Luke places the prediction by Jesus of the defection of Peter and the other disciples with the events that transpired in the upper room, while the other two evangelists represent it as taking place after the arrival on the Mount of Olives. Luke also makes certain additions to the narrative from his special source *L*.

This incident is exceedingly important for the purposes of this study because there is much that it reveals of the consciousness of Jesus concerning himself and his mission. It is especially significant in what it reveals as to Jesus' interpretation of his death; there is scarcely any incident in the life of Jesus that can approach this one in its value in this particular. Furthermore, this incident shows Jesus establishing a solemn rite, a rite peculiar to his ministry and avowedly interpretative of his mission, a rite to be forever observed by those who commit themselves to his cause. Obviously a rite of this nature, instituted under the peculiarly impressive circumstances surrounding the last meeting of Jesus with the twelve before his death, was carefully and deliberately formulated by him and must of necessity reflect with singular clarity the inner workings of his mind and the profound convictions of his soul. It shall not be our purpose to attempt an exhaustive interpretation of this significant self-revelation of Jesus in the upper room; such would not be appropriate to the limitations of this study; it shall be our aim only to sketch in broad outlines what the conduct and words of Jesus on this occasion revealed concerning his conviction concerning himself.

Our first task is to understand the careful plans that were made by Jesus for the celebration of this last Passover with the twelve. There was careful planning in the preparation for this event, just as there was careful planning in preparation for the royal entry. Just as the pre-arrangements for the royal entry have been misunderstood by many, so the pre-arrangements for the celebration of the Passover have been misunderstood.

All three of the Synoptics agree as to the manner in which the use of the upper room was secured. In the "first day of unleavened bread" (that is, the 14th of Nisan, the day on which the Passover lamb was killed), the disciples came to Jesus and asked him, "Where wilt thou that we go and prepare that thou mayest eat the passover?" It is then recorded that Jesus selected two of the disciples, identified by Luke as Peter and John, and instructed them thus: "Go ye into the city, and there shall meet you a man bearing a pitcher of water: follow him. And wheresoever he shall go in, say ye to the goodman of the house, The Master saith, Where is the guestchamber, where I shall eat the passover with my disciples? And he will shew you a large upper room furnished and prepared: there make ready for us." It is then recorded that "his disciples went forth, and came into the city, and found as he had said unto them: and they made ready the passover."

The reference to a man with a pitcher of water upon his head will strike the reader who is conversant with eastern customs as singular. Men do not carry pitchers of water upon their heads in the East; nor was it the custom for them to do so in the time of Jesus. The carrying of water was woman's task. The sight of a man with a pitcher of water upon his head would arrest attention; he could be spotted easily on a crowded street. Jesus had obviously agreed in advance with the owner of the house upon this unique method by which the two disciples could be brought to the chosen place in time to complete the necessary preparations, which included the purchase of the lamb, its slaying, the sacrifice of the blood of the animal upon the altar in the Temple, and the cooking of the lamb for eating at the feast. There had also been an agreement between Jesus and the owner of the house in which the Passover was to be eaten concerning the "password" which the disciples were to give in order that they might be admitted to the upper room to make preparation for the feast. They were to follow the man with the pitcher upon his head into the house and were to say to the head of the house, "The Master saith, Where is the guestchamber, where I shall eat the passover with my disciples?" This saying would gain entrance for them into the upper room and apprize the head of the house of the fact that Jesus and the twelve would accept the hospitality of his home as Jesus had planned.

Why should it have been necessary for Jesus to adopt such a method in preparing for the celebration of this Passover Feast with the twelve? The answer is the necessity for keeping Judas in ignorance of the place. Because of this necessity Jesus could not divulge the plans for the eating of the Passover with any of the disciples. In divulging the plans to others than Judas it would have been necessary to warn those who shared the secret against making it known to the traitor, which would have at once aroused upsetting speculations. Jesus was aware of Judas' intentions and doubtless knew that he had already approached the rulers with the offer to deliver his Master to them. Thus Jesus was under the necessity of maintaining secrecy about his movements, for had Judas known in advance the place at which the Passover was to be eaten he would have undoubtedly notified the rulers and they would have effected the arrest of Jesus in the upper room even before the eating of the Passover was well under way. It was this necessity of secrecy and restraint that was responsible in part for the exclamation of Jesus when at last he was reclining with the twelve about the Passover table: "With desire I have desired [*Epithumia epithumēsa*] to eat this passover with you before I suffer" (Luke 22:15).

The great care exercised by Jesus in preparing for the Passover under the restraint of secrecy and the strain of loneliness is strongly suggestive of the importance attached by him to this final meeting with the twelve in the upper room. His conduct in this epochal meeting, his words, the new rite established by him, can only reflect that which is nearest his heart and most suggestive of his mission.

We come at once to the most important revelation this significant meeting in the upper room affords concerning the consciousness of Jesus as to his person and mission. This is that Jesus sees himself in this meeting as bringing to a close the old sacrificial system in Israel and as founding a new covenant between God and his people. The old sacrificial system, represented in the sacrifice and Feast of the Passover, he sees fulfilled in this new covenant. In this epochal transition from an old to a new dispensation Jesus interprets his death as the effectuating cause, the central factor. He pictures his blood as the seal of this new covenant. As an everlasting memorial of this new covenant he founds the new Supper of the bread and the wine, the symbols of the giving of his body and blood to seal the covenant.

If all this was in the mind of Jesus when he met with the twelve in the upper room on the night before his crucifixion, two facts are at once apparent: (1) The position he takes with reference to himself is consistent with the unique and exalted place he has ascribed to himself all along, and is the natural development of the patterns to which he committed himself at the outset of his ministry. (2) The vast importance which he attaches to his death in effectuating a new relationship between God and man can only be the expression of sublime knowledge and profound conviction that were in him from the beginning of his ministry—it cannot be consistent with some recent purpose to die or some impulse to give himself to martyrdom in order to save his cause or bring in the Kingdom of God with power.

But let us see if we have judged correctly of what Jesus was thinking of himself and his mission on this memorable night. First of all, let it be determined whether or not Jesus conceived of himself as bringing to a close the old dispensation of sacrifice. Luke's narrative of the events in the upper room is suggestive at this point. He records the giving of two cups, one before and one after the bread was given. It is evident that Luke's first cup is the last cup of the Passover meal, the "cup of blessing" of the old feast. By this mention of the last cup of the Passover and by the quoting of Jesus' words in comment on the giving of the cup, Luke intends to show the nexus of the old feast with the new, and the fulfilment of the old in the new. To this end he quotes the words of Jesus at the giving of this cup: "Take this, and divide it among yourselves: For I say unto you, I will not drink from henceforth of the fruit of the vine until the kingdom of God shall come" (22:17f.). The evangelist has put these words in the mouth of Jesus at this point to show that he was in the act of celebrating the Passover for the last time, not because his death would prevent his observing the Feast again, but because when he drank of the "fruit of the vine" again with his disciples it would be when the Kingdom of God had "come." Now since Luke goes on to show that within a few minutes after uttering these words Jesus did drink of the "fruit of the vine" again in the second cup mentioned by the evangelist, it is clear that Luke interprets the institution of the new Supper, the "Lord's Supper," as signalizing a "coming" of the Kingdom of God. His view is that when Jesus drank the "fruit of the vine" in this second cup, he was drinking it in the dispensation of the Kingdom of God. Thus Luke's narrative makes clear what is implicit in the narratives of Mark and Matthew:

that Jesus conceived of the Passover as ceasing and as being fulfilled in this new Supper of the Kingdom of God.

To grasp the significance of this conviction of Jesus that on this night in an upper room in Jerusalem with twelve men about him he was bringing to a close the historic dispensation of Jewish sacrifices and was establishing a new covenant, it is profitable to remember the meaning of the Passover Feast. The Passover had its roots deep in the life and culture of the Hebrew people. It was established before the law was given and before the covenant was sealed at Sinai. It was the heart of the sacrificial system. Established as it was at the deliverance of the Israelites from the bondage of Egypt it remained an everlasting memorial of salvation and deliverance. It was never to be forgotten that it was the blood of the first Passover lambs that marked the houses of the people of Jehovah when the angel of death passed through Egypt. It was the blood of the lambs, the people of Israel understood, that kept the angel of death from their homes. Thus the concept of the efficacy of sacrifice and blood for deliverance and salvation was at the heart of the philosophy of the Passover. The Feast was always the chief feast of the Jews. It was one of the two feasts that all males of Israel twenty years of age and over were expected to attend. The celebration of the Feast was surrounded with meticulous regulations that were to be scrupulously obeyed. The lamb for the Passover was to be carefully selected; it was to be without blemish—this because its blood shed upon the altar was symbolic of the life of the people as belonging to Jehovah. In the communal eating of the lamb there was the strong suggestion of the presence of Jehovah with his people, of the communion of the people through this sacrifice, with God.

Now Jesus claims for himself the authority to abolish this Feast and institute another, the new to be the fulfilment of the old. Surely he sees himself as a unique person in the history of Israel in this conviction that he is vested with such authority! But in what manner is the new feast to supplant the old, and what will this new covenant offer as substitute for the sacrifice of the Passover? The record is very clear concerning what was in the mind of Jesus. The Synoptics all agree in substance to his words, although the slight additions to the primary source made by Matthew and Luke are significant, as we shall see. Mark, the primary source, gives the story thus:

> And as they did eat, Jesus took bread, and blessed, and brake it, and gave it to them, and said, Take eat: this is my body. And he took the cup, and when he had given thanks, he gave it to them: and they all drank of it. And he said unto them, This is my blood of the new testament, which is shed for many. Verily I say unto you, I will drink no more of the fruit of the vine, until that day that I drink it new in the kingdom of God.

We shall take notice of the additions of Matthew and Luke. Matthew reports Jesus as saying, when he gave the bread, "Take, *eat,*" and saying when he gave the cup: "This is my blood of the covenant [not *new* covenant as some texts have it], which is shed for many *for the remission of sins.*" Luke reports that Jesus said when he gave the bread: "This is my body *which is given for you: this do in remembrance of me.* Likewise also the cup after supper, saying, This cup is the *new* testament in my blood, which is shed for you." Westcott and Hort in their text place brackets around all of this statement beginning with "which is given for you," classifying all this part of the narrative as an "interpolation" on the ground of its being omitted by "Western" documents. Such an omission, however, would leave Luke without any mention at all of the cup of the Lord's Supper, and it is not likely that this would truly represent Luke's autograph. The confusion in the manuscripts arose no doubt because of Luke's independent handling of the source material and his design of mentioning the last cup of the Passover as well as the cup of the new Supper. The evidence is insufficient to classify this portion of the narrative as an "interpolation"; if it is omitted by the "Western" documents it is included in the more important "Neutral" family of documents. The additions of Luke are certainly not inconsistent with the ideas of Jesus as presented in the Markan narrative. His "This is my body *which is given for you*" is more specific than Mark's "Take eat, this is my body" and Matthew's "Take, eat; this is my body," but the truth of what Luke adds is implicit in the invitation of Jesus to the disciples to "take" or to "take" and "eat" his body, for certainly if the disciples take and eat the body it is *given for* them. Luke's description of the cup as "the cup of the *new* testament in my blood, which is shed for you" and Mark's "This is my blood of the new testament, which is shed for many," and Matthew's "This is my blood of the covenant which is shed for many for the remission of sins" are in essential agreement in principle. Luke's statement designates the covenant as *new,* a fact that is obvious in the other narratives, since any covenant established by Jesus would be a new covenant. Matthew and Mark make a universal application of the statement of Jesus (the blood is shed for *many*), and Matthew is more specific in designating the purpose of the shedding of the blood; according to this Evangelist the blood is shed for *many,* and the purpose of the shedding of the blood is "for the remission of sins." We repeat that there is no basic disagreement in the narratives; each evangelist presents in his own way a claim which if true is of staggering importance and cosmic significance, namely, the claim of a person called Jesus, a Galilean carpenter, that he has the right to abolish the ancient and important feast of the Jews called the Passover, and by implication the right to put an end to the whole sacrificial system of the Jewish nation; that by giving himself in death the intent of the sacrificial system will be realized and thus the Passover and all other sacrifices will no longer be necessary, and that by the act of his death he will provide that which is necessary for the "remission of sins" of "many." That one man should make a claim of such magnitude for himself, or that he should reveal an idea of such staggering implications as belonging to his consciousness is a matter in itself to arrest attention and demand explanation. This is not the place to discuss the validity of Jesus' claims or the question of the corroboration of these claims in the verdict of history. It is worthwhile simply to observe in passing that the historical work of Jesus and the position which history accords him are justifiable grounds for the view that the conviction he entertained concerning his person and mission is consistent with reality and with the facts of history.

What, then, was Jesus' view of himself on this memorable night in the upper room? He said as he gave the bread, "This is my body." That is to say, the bread represented his body. Since the bread was to be eaten, the implication is that his body is to be eaten in a figurative sense. That is to say, it is to be received and appropriated by his disciples. This is a way of saying that his body will take the place of the body of the Passover lamb. He, then, will become the Passover Lamb. As the Passover lamb dies and becomes a sacrifice, he will die and become a sacrifice; and as the body of the Passover lamb is eaten, so his body must be "eaten." That is, he in his death must be received and appropriated by his disciples. And now he says of the cup as he gives it to the disciples, "This is my blood of the covenant, which is shed for many." The mind of Jesus now passes to the giving of the old covenant, that memorable occasion when Israel was constituted a nation as the people stood at the foot of Mount Sinai and made solemn promise that they would do all that the Lord said they must do. "And Moses wrote all the words of the Lord," the record goes, "and rose up early in the morning, and builded an altar under the hill, and twelve pillars, according to the twelve tribes of Israel. . . . And Moses took half of the blood, and put it in basins; and half of the blood he sprinkled on the altar. And he took the book of the covenant, and read it in the audience of the people: and they said, All that the Lord hath said will we do, and be obedient. And Moses took the blood, and sprinkled it on the people, and said, Behold the blood of the covenant which the Lord hath made with you concerning all these words" (Exodus 24:4-8). Luke correctly interprets the mind of Jesus when he quotes him as saying, "This is the *new* testament in my blood." Jesus sees himself on this night as establishing a new covenant between God and man; but more, he sees himself as constituting through this covenant a *new* nation, the *new Israel.* This new covenant between God and man which makes possible the constitution of a new nation, a new Israel, is to be sealed with the blood of Jesus himself. This he plainly says. The old covenant was sealed with the blood of animals, the new will be sealed with the blood of a person. But surely in the very suggestion that the blood of a person could seal a covenant between God and man, that would constitute a new nation, there is implicit the truth that the person whose blood is used to seal the covenant is no ordinary individual. Jesus knows that as he makes this great claim of the efficacy of his blood that he must be more than mortal man in order to provide blood so precious. A new covenant between God and man, a new nation thereby established, forgiveness for all men in one sacrifice—whose blood but the blood of the Son of God could seal a covenant so great?

This blood of which the wine in the cup is the symbol is "shed for many," or, as Matthew has it, "for many for the remission [forgiveness] of sins." The expression "for many" undoubtedly points to the universal efficacy of the blood of Jesus. The blood of the animals in the ancient sacrificial system was effective in providing atonement for the faithful Israelite, but not for the Gentile. Jesus saw the shedding of his blood as of universal significance; through his blood there would be forgiveness of sins for *many*; that is, for all men in all history. Jesus is interpreting redemption and atonement; he is saying that in his death he will do for men what the sacrifice of animals could not do, what men could never do for themselves: provide atonement for sins. He does not explain the mystery of atonement—he announces his power to provide it. In the revelation that he makes of his authority to secure for all men forgiveness of sins by the shedding of his blood, Jesus is again exhibiting his true Sonship to God. He is acting as the Son who truly reveals the Father and he is maintaining the fidelity he has shown all along to the knowledge of the character of God he manifested in his victory over Satan in the wilderness of Judea. There he acted as the Son of God who is redeeming love; here in the upper room he shows what the God who is redeeming love will do that all men may be reconciled to him: he will give his Son as a sacrifice that men may be redeemed from their sins. But there is this that man must do: he must appropriate the sacrifice, he must eat the bread which is the body of Christ.

Jesus is conscious, we have said, that he is constituting a new nation, the new Israel, through the giving of this new covenant sealed with his blood. In this he sees himself as the Messiah of the Remnant of Israel. Here are his twelve apostles before him; they represent the twelve tribes of Israel and the Remnant of the Chosen People. How otherwise could Jesus establish a new covenant unless there was the "Remnant" of Israel present with whom the new covenant might be made? Jesus was familiar with the doctrine of the Remnant and there is every reason to believe that he accepted the idea of the Remnant as essential to the fulfilment of his mission. He had foreseen and predicted his rejection by the leaders of the nation. How, then, would his work be saved? Through the Remnant of Israel. It would be the Remnant that would accept him as Messiah, conserve his teachings and propagate his gospel to the point where the Gentiles would receive it and carry it on to all the world. It would be through the acceptance of his Messiahship by the Remnant, and through the work of the Remnant, that the ancient prophecies would be fulfilled and the age-long dealing of Jehovah with his people vindicated. Jesus knew that the prophets had spoken of the Remnant of Israel that would return to Jehovah and be saved. Jeremiah had said: "And I will gather the remnant of my flock out of all countries whither I have driven them, and will bring them again to their folds; and they shall be fruitful and increase. And I will set up shepherds over them which shall feed them: and they shall fear no more, nor be dismayed, neither shall they be lacking, saith the Lord. Behold, the days come, saith the Lord, that I will raise unto David a righteous Branch, and a King shall reign and prosper, and shall execute judgment and justice in the earth. In his days Judah shall be saved, and Israel shall dwell safely: and this is his name whereby he shall be called, The Lord Our Righteousness" (23:3-6).

Gathered with these twelve men of Israel on this night before his crucifixion Jesus was indeed with the "Remnant" of Israel. We may believe that he saw himself as this righteous Branch of David of whom Jeremiah spoke, standing in the midst of the "Remnant" of Jehovah's flock, establishing with this Remnant a new covenant and constituting thereby a new Israel so that the prophecy would come to pass that "Judah shall be saved, and Israel shall dwell safely."

V. Gethsemane

(Mark 14:32-42; Matthew 26:36-46; Luke 22:39-46)

The primary source of the narrative is Mark.

It is necessary to seek light on the mystery of Gethsemane if we are to be loyal to our quest for knowledge of the mind of Jesus in this final week of his ministry. It is beyond the limits of this study to pursue in detail the meaning of Jesus' conduct in the garden of Gethsemane, but there is one question that challenges our attention. If a reasonable answer to this question can be found, some contribution shall have been made to an understanding of the consciousness of Jesus concerning himself as he stands in the awful shadow of the cross. The question is "Why did Jesus act as he did in the immediate prospect of his death? What is revealed in the admission to his disciples, "My soul is exceeding sorrowful unto death?" What is the meaning of the agonizing prayer, "O my Father, if it be possible, let this cup pass away from me"? Why the manifestations of anguish in the falling on the ground as he prayed?

The conduct of Jesus in the face of his own death is extraordinary. Is this obvious shrinking from the ordeal ahead of him the manifestation of fear and weakness? How can one who has walked so bravely through life act thus as he faces death?

A common explanation of the conduct of Jesus in Gethsemane is that his agony and suffering were due to his human nature; it was the frailty of the flesh that caused him to act as he did, it is said. But this explanation is unsatisfactory when it is recalled that so many mortals have faced death with poise and equanimity. Thousands of young men daily face death in time of war with a casualness that is often startling. Even criminals approach execution in a mood of stolid indifference. It is interesting in this connection to remember the conduct of Socrates as he drank his cup of hemlock.

Phaedo, in reporting to his friends on the happenings of the fateful day on which Socrates died, is quoted by Plato as saying:

> For myself, the feelings I experienced there beside him were amazing. Within I felt no pity such as I might feel when present at the death of a dear friend, for to me, Echecrates, he seemed to be a happy man, alike in his bearing and his words, so fearlessly and nobly did he meet his end; so that he struck me, even on his way to Hades, as one who went, not without divine allotment, but, if ever man did, to fare well on his arrival there.[2]

Coming to the end of his story where he describes how Socrates accepted the cup, Phaedo continues:

> With that he handed Socrates the cup. He took it, and Echecrates, quite cheerfully, without a tremor or any change of color, or alteration in his face, but looking at the man askance in his ironic fashion, asked: "What say you? Is it lawful that we make libation from this beverage to a god? Or must we not?" "Socrates," he said, "we prepare no more than what we think will be the right amount." "I understand," he answered. "But, at all events, no doubt I may, I must, pray to the gods that my change of abode from hence to the world beyond shall be attended by success. That is my prayer; so be it!" So saying, he put the cup to his lips, and with great ease, without the least aversion, he drained the contents down.[3]

And now contrast with this the Gospel narrative of the experience of Jesus in the garden of Gethsemane:

> And he taketh with him Peter and James and John, and began to be sore amazed, and to be very heavy; and saith unto them, My soul is exceeding sorrowful unto death: tarry ye here, and watch. And he went forward a little, and fell on the ground, and prayed that, if it were possible, the hour might pass from him. And he said, Abba, Father, all things are possible unto thee; take away this cup from me: nevertheless not what I will, but what thou wilt (Mark 14:33-36).

---

[2] From *Plato On the Trial and Death of Socrates*, translated by Lane Cooper, Cornell University Press, Ithaca, p. 112. By permission.

[3] *Op. cit.*, p. 191 f. By permission.

How great the contrast in the manner in which Socrates received his cup and that in which Jesus received his! Here before us are the portraits of two great and good men as they faced their deaths! How amazingly different they are! Somehow we feel that multitudes of good men would approach their deaths in the manner of Socrates, not of Jesus. The conduct of Jesus was extraordinary; the conduct of Socrates that of the good and wise man in any age as he approaches death. What is the explanation of the singular conduct of Jesus?

A clue to the solution of the mystery is to be found, we believe, in something that Socrates said and in something that Jesus said as each faced death. Both men were religious and both men faced God as they came to the final hour of life. Accommodating himself to the polytheistic notions of the time, Socrates remarked: "But, at all events, no doubt I may, I must, pray to the gods that my change of abode from hence to the world beyond shall be attended by success." Socrates reveals in his remark no consciousness of even a personal relationship between himself and the gods. But hear the cry of Jesus: "Abba, Father, all things are possible unto thee; take away this cup from me." To Jesus God is one God, but more, he is *Father!* The retention of the Aramaic word for Father, *Abba,* suggests further Jesus' consciousness of his intensely personal relationship to God—God is *his* Father. Matthew has him saying, "O *my* Father." The sum of the matter is that Jesus is conscious of his Sonship to God in the garden of Gethsemane. He agonizes and struggles in the face of death, not because of his humanity, but because he is the Son of God!

But why should Jesus' Sonship cause him to act thus in the presence of his death? First of all, because his death is a seeming contradiction of his Sonship. The ordeal of death is therefore a test of his faith, his faith in God, his faith in his own consciousness of his unique relationship to God. His soul becomes the battlefield of a terrific struggle, the struggle between the awful reality of death and the conviction that he is the Son of God. Of course, his human nature is involved in the struggle, for he is one person, not two. As the awful struggle begins he enters into the deep realization of the demands of that other office he has chosen for himself, the office of the Suffering Servant of Jehovah.

Again, Jesus' Sonship causes him to suffer as none other has suffered in the presence of death because of the spiritual sensitivity that of necessity was a part of that nature which sustained a unique relationship to God. As the Son he was conscious of his innocence of wrong-doing, and yet he knew that on the morrow he would die as a malefactor; as the Son he was conscious that he had brought to his nation and to the life of mankind its purest ray of hope and its most glorious holiness, and yet he knew that he was "despised and rejected of men." The sensitivity of his soul, sharpened far beyond the spiritual sensitivity of the average man, enabled him to feel the hard thrusts of sin in a way that other men could never feel them.

This is why Jesus acted as he did in the garden of Gethsemane. And when he returned to the sleeping disciples for the last time and saw the band of evil men approaching to arrest him, he said, "behold, the *Son of man* is betrayed into the hands of sinners." The agony of the garden has not shaken his faith in his conviction that he is the great Son of Man whose power in time will prevail and whose coming in glory will vindicate the sufferings of the Son of God upon the earth.

VI. The Arrest and Trials

(Mark 14:43–15:23; Matthew 26:47–27:34; Luke 22:47–23:33)

Mark is the primary source. Matthew and Luke supplement the passion narratives with use of independent sources.

Our purpose in following Jesus through his arrest and trials will be to observe his conduct in order to discover what it reveals of his consciousness concerning himself. Jesus now passes under the control of others. These are evil men, and for the most part men who hate him, men bent upon destroying him. This is an entirely new situation for Jesus; heretofore he has been the master of his own movements, but from the moment he surrenders himself to his enemies in the garden of Gethsemane until he breathes his last upon the cross he is a prisoner, under the coercion and control of others. What are his thoughts as he passes under the control of men of evil will? What does he think of himself and his mission as he moves into the heart of the stronghold of sin he has been facing these many months? Does he reveal himself to be the Son of God when the impact of the storm breaks upon him? Is he faithful to his character as the Suffering Servant of Jehovah?

The present discussion calls for no detailed study of the arrest and trials. It is only necessary to pause for a brief glance at Jesus as he faces each of the important crises in this series of events, in order to determine the nature of his convictions about himself.

First of all, we turn our attention to the conduct of Jesus as the band sent by the religious leaders came to arrest him in the garden. He meets this ordeal with rare self-possession and dignity. His question to the traitor is, "Judas, betrayest thou the Son of man with a kiss?" (Luke 22:48.) His use of the title Son of Man in this situation is suggestive of his thinking in this critical moment in which he passes into the control of evil men. Betrayed by one of his own disciples, it is a source of wonderment to him that the traitor could by a token indicating respect and loyalty (the kissing of the hand of a master by a disciple) betray him who is the great Son of Man. Loyalty such as the kiss implied could never permit the betrayal of the Son of Man in such fashion. Thus we see that Jesus is fully conscious of his exalted position as he submits himself to arrest. He is in no wise conscious that he is betraying the office of Son of Man, or in any way compromising the character of this great personage, in allowing himself to be arrested.

One of the twelve undertook to defend Jesus by force. John identifies this disciple as Peter (18:10). The reaction of Jesus to this well-meaning demonstration of loyalty is significant. According to Matthew's narrative Jesus said to Peter: "Put up again thy sword into his place: for all they that take the sword shall perish with the sword. Thinkest thou that I cannot now pray to my Father, and he shall presently give me more than twelve legions of angels? But how then shall the scriptures be fulfilled, that thus it must be?" (26:52-54.) The conduct of Jesus as he actually faces the use of force in his own behalf is determined by his character as Messiah and by the renunciation he had made in the wilderness of Judea when he refused Satan's offer of the kingdoms of the earth in exchange for compromise with Satan. To have accepted the use of violence in his behalf in this crisis in the garden would have amounted to compromise with Satan and disloyalty to his great renunciation. Jesus explains to Peter the practical side of his principle when he declares that "all they that take the sword shall perish with the sword." In standing for a spiritual Kingdom Jesus has assured the indestructibility and universality of the Kingdom by freeing it from the limitations peculiar to earthly kingdoms; earthly kingdoms limit themselves by the use of violence for their preservation, for by the employment of violence they bring against themselves the use of violence and thereby subject themselves to destruction by violence. As a spiritual Kingdom the Kingdom of God can employ only spiritual weapons. It is a gross injustice, therefore, to the clear teaching of Jesus to advocate the use of violence to defend or propagate the Kingdom of God. Jesus was not approaching the ordeal of arrest in the spirit of helplessness. He was never more conscious of his power. The power of the Spirit, the power of love, were never more dramatically displayed than in Jesus' rebuke to Peter in the garden. Conscious of the fact that he might have had twelve legions of angels as his defenders, conscious that he might have had the protection of a thousand swords in the hands of as many loyal partisans, he commands Peter to sheath his sword and goes forth to meet his enemies in the power of immortal love and in the spirit of the Suffering Servant of Jehovah.

And now Jesus stands before the Sanhedrin, the supreme court of Israel. Evil and sin express themselves in abundant measure in this meeting. It is an illegal gathering of the nation's highest tribunal because it is held before dawn and because the meeting place is at the house of Caiaphas and not in the council chamber. False witnesses are used in the trial. In the face of all this he maintains an eloquent and dignified silence. According to Mark "he held his peace, and answered nothing" (14:61). Only when put upon oath and asked by the high priest the direct question, "Art thou the Christ, the Son of the Blessed?" did he speak. Then with simple and devastating frankness, easily understood by the men of the court, he replied: "I am," adding as evidence of the consciousness of his dignity and certain vindication, even as he stood before the leaders of Israel a prisoner: "and ye shall see the Son of man sitting on the right hand of power, and coming in the clouds of heaven" (Mark 14:61f.). When all the pent-up venom was loosed upon him and these dignitaries begin to spit in his face and strike him with their hands, and challenge him to prophesy," he says nothing. He who has just confessed himself to be the Son of God is in truth that Servant of whom the prophet said: "He was oppressed, and he was afflicted, yet he opened not his mouth: he is brought as a lamb to the slaughter, and as a sheep before her shearers is dumb, so he openeth not his mouth."

The undying love that never left him in all these trying hours, manifested in one unforgettable and soul-searching glance, was sufficient to break the heart of Simon Peter when after the third denial Jesus turned and looked into the face of his faltering disciple. Sorrow, love, forgiveness were mingled in that glance. When Peter's eyes met those of Jesus he "went out and wept bitterly" (Luke 22:61f.).

Jesus maintained the dignity of silence before the Roman governor, Pilate, according to the Synoptic records, with one exception. He replied to the governor's question, "Art thou the King of the Jews?" His answer was, "Thou sayest" (Mark 15:2). By this reply Jesus in effect said, "You are saying what I am," that is to say, he acknowledged to Pilate that he was the King of the Jews. This is a revelation of his unchanged conviction that he is the son of David, the true Messiah. This conviction, stoutly maintained under the circumstances that would belie every semblance of the validity of his claim to be King, convincingly attests his faith in the spiritual messianic pattern. Standing, a prisoner, before this vacillating and corrupt official who has in his hands the power to release him, Jesus confidently affirms his Kingship. He knows full well he is a king of the sort that Pilate does not know. He is King of the Jews, yes, but he would not be standing here a prisoner if he conformed himself to the Jewish concept of king; it is because he is in truth *the* King of the Jews, the son of David's line whose kingdom would be universal and eternal, that he stands a prisoner before Pilate's judgment seat. When the chief priests accused Jesus of "many things" to Pilate he "no more answered anything, so that Pilate marvelled" (Mark 15:3-5).

The same dignified silence was maintained by Jesus when he was sent by Pilate to Herod Antipas and was compelled to listen to the meaningless questions of this wicked puppet. "He answered him nothing" and bore in silence the horseplay to which he was subjected by Herod and his soldiers when they dressed him in royal robes and mocked him (Luke 23:6-12). Delivered up at last by Pilate to be crucified, Jesus was given the cruel Roman scourging to which criminals were subjected before crucifixion and was placed in the hands of Roman soldiers. These callous, uncouth men dressed him in purple, put a crown of thorns upon his head, mocked him because of his claim to be a king, and spit on him. But Jesus remained silent as this crude and cruel treatment was heaped upon him. Never was there a king who exercised such power as this! Jesus sat upon a throne of love and wielded the scepter of spiritual might. Caught in this base display of brutality, his consciousness of his kingly majesty is manifest in his conduct. Here indeed he arises to the full stature of that one of whom Isaiah spoke when he said: "He is despised and rejected of men; a man of sorrows, and acquainted with grief: and we hid as it were our faces from him; he was despised, and we esteemed him not. Surely he hath borne our griefs, and carried our sorrows: Yet we did esteem him stricken, smitten of God, and afflicted. But he was wounded for our transgressions, he was bruised for our iniquities: the chastisement of our peace was upon him; and with his stripes we are healed."

On the way to Calvary Jesus observed the weeping of the women who followed him on the painful journey. His reaction to this is significant. He tells them not to weep for him but "for yourselves, and for your children." He is thinking of the terrible days ahead, of the coming sorrows of Jerusalem, and of the awful implication of the tragic events that center now about his rejection. Again he is conscious of the epochal nature of his mission and of the vast significance of the rejection of their Messiah by the leaders of the nation. "For if they do these things in the green tree, what shall be done in the dry?" Jesus asks of the weeping women as he trudges the painful path to the summit of Golgotha (Luke 23:31). The meaning of his question is that his advent, his ministry, his offer of the Kingdom are the "green tree," which constitute Israel's epochal opportunity to fulfil the demands of its mission. If the leaders fail to recognize this tree of opportunity when it is green, what is to be expected of them when the tree stands stark and denuded of its leaves?

When at last the procession came to the top of the hill Jesus was offered wine mingled with myrrh before he was impaled upon his cross. This was a narcotic, its offer being the one compassionate touch evident in the whole cruel business of execution by crucifixion. Its purpose was to alleviate in some degree the terrible physical pain which a crucified person suffered. When Jesus perceived that it was the customary narcotic that was being offered to him, he refused to drink it. It was his desire to go through the horrible ordeal to the bitter end in full possession of his faculties. He was conscious that even upon this cross upon which he would hang he would be the representative of God and the mouthpiece of divine love. His conduct and his words must express clearly, even to the last breath, the meaning of that love. Indeed, as the storm of sin beats about his head in one great final blast and the fiends of hell shriek with delight at his dying agonies, there will come the climactic test of his faith in himself and of his trust in God, and there will be given to him the greatest opportunity of all to reveal his Sonship and the meaning of redemptive love. Melted in the fires of his last great test, every word from his lips will be freighted with meaning of eternal significance.

And so Jesus enters the climactic test in full possession of his faculties and firm in the conviction that he is both the King of the Jews and the Son of God. But he knows likewise that he is in truth the Servant of Jehovah as he is impaled upon his cross.

VII. On the Cross

(Mark 15:24-37; Matthew 27:35-50; Luke 23:33-46)

Again the primary source is Mark, but we find significant and valuable additions by Luke from his special source. Of the four sayings from the cross recorded by the Synoptics, three are given by Luke.

The first utterance of Jesus, according to Luke, was the prayer for forgiveness: "Father, forgive them; for they know not what they do." It was for the soldiers whose duty it was to crucify him and who gambled at the foot of his cross for his garments that Jesus uttered this prayer. These men were unaware that they were participating in the execution of an innocent man. The great compassion of Jesus for humanity, especially his compassion for the little people, the underprivileged, the poor, is manifested in this prayer. His heart goes out to these rude men, callous perhaps, but unaware of the magnitude of the crime in which they are innocent participants. *Father* as the name for God is still upon the lips of Jesus; there is still the consciousness in the one who is dying upon this cross of the nearness of God and of the unique relationship which he sustains to him. In this prayer for forgiveness of ignorant sinners there is the revelation of the knowledge of divine love that only the Son could make. Only the Son could know that in an hour of anguish so great love must beg forgiveness for those who inflicted the pain.

Once again Luke records an utterance that echoes the height and depth of redemptive love. It is the word of

Jesus to the repentant robber who had asked that Jesus would remember him when he came into his kingdom. The answer of Jesus was: "Today shalt thou be with me in paradise." By this reply he confirms the robber's confession that he was the possessor of a Kingdom. He hung as a criminal upon a cross, and this was in tragic contrast with the glad days in Galilee when he preached the good tidings of the Kingdom and men thronged him and hung upon his words as he told them of the Kingdom's mysteries. His faith in that Kingdom is not dead because he hangs upon this cross; rather he hangs upon this cross because he believed in the Kingdom. The robber has sensed the truth that he is indeed the King-Messiah and he has faith that his Kingdom will "come." The anguish of this terrible moment cannot stem the tide of redemptive love as it proceeds from God the Father through Jesus the Son to encompass the soul of a poor dying criminal. How clear is Jesus' consciousness of the great authority his Father has given him! Who but the Son could believe there was a paradise at all as he hung in shame upon a Roman cross, dying, not because he was bad, but because he was supremely good? The certainty of Jesus' conviction that he was the Son and that power of redemption had been given into his hands was never more apparent than in this sublime answer to the malefactor by his side: "Today shalt thou be with me in paradise."

After six anguished hours had dragged by and Jesus came at last to the very portal of death he cried out in anguish "My God, my God, why hast thou forsaken me?" The words are recorded by Mark and Matthew and belong to the primitive tradition. There is no doubt that Jesus uttered them. What do they signify? Do they reveal that in the end Jesus lost his faith because God failed to come to his rescue and deliver him from the cross? Was it true that he expected God to perform a miracle in rescuing him from the cross before death, and the cry of desolation was the expression of bitter disappointment that his Father had failed him? Surely if the evangelists who recorded these words believed that this was the explanation of this cry of desolation they would have hesitated to preserve them. Especially it seems that Matthew would have been loath to include them in his narrative in view of his preservation of the claim of Jesus in the garden that he might have had twelve legions of angels as defenders only by praying to his Father for them (26:53), for why should Jesus expect deliverance on the cross when he renounced it in the garden? No, this was not a cry of disappointment—it was a cry of anguish. It was the expression of the Son's most acute moment of suffering, the moment that brought him to the dark portal of death. The cry was the spontaneous expression of agony that could come only from the soul of the Son of God as he became aware that the moment had arrived for his passage through that portal. Again it is profitable to contrast the dying of Socrates with that of Jesus. Phaedo describes for his friends the end of his great master thus:

> Already he was growing cold below the navel, when he uncovered his face—for he had covered it—and spoke—they were his last words: "Crito," he said, "we owe a cock to Aesculapius; you must not forget to pay it." "It shall be done," said Crito. Can you think of anything else?" To this question he made no reply; but in a little while there was a convulsive movement, after which the man uncovered him. His eyes were fixed. When Crito saw, he closed the mouth and eyes.[4]

The reference of Socrates to Aesculapius is interesting. He was the god of medicine, and the meaning of Socrates' remark is that he owes to this god the sacrifice of a cock because through the hemlock the god has made possible the liberation of Socrates' soul from the body. Socrates displays the poise and self-control of a wise and good man as he comes to die. He is sincerely grateful to whatever gods there may be for the peace that comes to him. He does not forget the patron god of medicine, and remembers with characteristic humor the "debt" he owes to him because of his gift of hemlock. How different is the death of Jesus! He cries out as he comes to the last moment of life: "My God, my God, why hast thou forsaken me?" It is because he is so much more than Socrates that Jesus speaks thus in

---

[4] From *Plato On the Trial and Death of Socrates*, translated by Lane Cooper, Cornell University Press, p. 192. By permission.

his moment of approach to death. It is because he is conscious of his Sonship, because as the Son he is keenly sensitive to the meaning of death, because he sees the significance of the death of the Son of God that he utters this cry of desolation.

The cry does not mean that he believes that God has severed himself from his Son. It means that he is puzzled and baffled that the Father should abandon the Son to die. "Why did you forsake me?" (the verb is Aorist, not perfect) means "Why did you forsake me to the point of allowing me to die?" It is not that Jesus has lost his consciousness of the necessity of his death, but that he voices the depth of the anguish that fills his soul because it is necessary for the Father to abandon him to death.

But this is not the last word. Luke tells us of one last utterance that fell from his lips. It was: "Father, into thy hands I commend my spirit." It was after he said this that he breathed his last. Again he comes to the word he knew best as he thinks of addressing God. Socrates may humorously speak of a debt he owes to the god of medicine as he approaches the end, but Jesus speaks of the one God who is Father and addresses him in such manner as to reveal the consciousness that he sustains a unique relationship with him. It is vastly significant that as the breath leaves his body at the end of his awful experience of suffering he can think of God as Father. It is good to know that although he cried out, "My God, my God, why?" he addressed God in the end as "Father." Surely this is an exhibition of perfect faith and perfect love! It was as the Son that he cried out, "My God, my God, why?" but it was also as the Son that he said, "Father, into thy hands I commend my spirit."

It was the Suffering Servant of Jehovah who scaled the hill called Calvary and was crucified there. But in his suffering and death the Servant was also the Son of God and the Son of Man, *because redemption was wrought out on that hill!*

VII

BEYOND CALVARY

The object of this book is to bring to light from the consciousness of Jesus the truth of the opinion that he held concerning himself and his mission. The quest which we began in the wilderness of Judea led step by step to Calvary. But if the story ends there, of what profit is the knowledge of Jesus' estimate of himself?

One of the surest proofs of all that the story did not end on Calvary is the continuing influence of Jesus in history. Presently we shall see that this continuing influence of Jesus in history is of a different character from that of other great men and religious leaders who also live on in history through influence. Our immediate concern is with the resurrection of Jesus. But the point is now made that Jesus could not have achieved the unique position he occupied in history had the disciples not been convinced that he lived after his tragic death by crucifixion. The point has been argued ably many times and there is no necessity for repeating it here. Suffice it to say that the disciples were convinced, contrary to their expectations, that Jesus did rise from the dead, and that it was the knowledge that he was alive that restored their confidence in him and transformed their crushing defeat into an amazing resurgence of life and energy that propelled the Christian movement into the Graeco-Roman world as a part of the stream of history.

Furthermore, it should be said that the resurrection is necessary for the completion of the picture of Jesus. By the picture of Jesus we mean the picture that he drew of himself as Son of God and universal Saviour. This was the picture that the disciples accepted after the resurrection; it was the only picture of Jesus which the apostle

Paul knew, and it is the picture that has sustained Christianity as a historical movement through the centuries. The resurrection is necessary to this picture, we say. It is necessary because it belongs to the estimate which Jesus made of himself during his ministry. We have seen that he believed and taught that he would arise from the dead. It is impossible, therefore, to separate this conviction that he would arise from the dead from the other beliefs he held concerning himself without doing violence to his total self-consciousness. The conviction that he would arise from the dead is part and parcel of Jesus' consciousness that he was the Son of God.

The resurrection is also necessary to the picture of Jesus because of the logic of the incarnation. The early disciples were right in conceiving of the resurrection as a validation of Jesus as the Son of God. *It cannot be that death has dominion over the Son!* Jesus cannot be conceived of as the incarnation of God if he did not arise from the dead. Death cannot hold the Spirit of the living God.

The story does not end with Calvary. We proceed, therefore, to examine the Synoptic records with a view to finding what is significant for our study in the words and conduct of Jesus after he rose from the dead.

I. The Mind of the Risen Christ

Admittedly the records are brief. In keeping with the method observed in this study, John's Gospel cannot be utilized. Further limitation is placed upon the sources of data because of the unavailability of Mark 16:9-20, which must be rejected because it is not contained in the great uncial manuscripts Aleph and B, and because it fails to meet the test of textual criticism. The loss of this spurious ending of Mark's Gospel is gain. It adds nothing of value that is not contained in the other Gospels and attributes to Jesus certain statements that sound very strange in his mouth. It should be pointed out, however, that Mark does give his testimony to the empty tomb in 16:1-8.

For words and acts of Jesus that reveal his thinking

after his resurrection, we must rely upon the narratives in Matthew and Luke. The passages are Matthew 28:9-10 and 16-20 and Luke 24:13-35 and 36-49. Each author drew from his own independent source for the narratives containing the passages cited from his Gospel.

Drawing from these passages, it shall be our aim to show briefly what was uppermost in the mind of Jesus during the forty days that he appeared to the disciples after his resurrection.

1. *Jesus wished the disciples to know beyond peradventure of doubt that he who came to them after his death was the same Jesus they had known before his crucifixion.* When he met the women as they were on their way to tell the disciples that they had found the tomb empty, he said to them, "Be not afraid: go tell my brethren that they go into Galilee, and there shall they see me" (Matthew 28:10). The women had recognized him as Jesus (Matthew 28:9). His exhortation to them to "cease fearing" (*mē phobeisthe*) indicated his desire that they should receive him as Jesus and not think of him as a spirit or an apparition. In his appearance to Cleopas and the other with whom he walked to Emmaus, Jesus conducted himself in such fashion while he sat at table and broke bread and gave to his hosts that "their eyes were opened, and they knew him" (Luke 24:30f.). Later, when he appeared to the eleven in Jerusalem and they were terrified because they thought he was a spirit, Jesus said, "Why are ye troubled? and why do thoughts arise in your hearts? Behold my hands and my feet, that it is I myself: handle me, and see; for a spirit hath not flesh and bones, as ye see me have" (Luke 24:37-39). Luke then relates how he showed them his hands and his feet and ate a piece of broiled fish and "of an honeycomb" in their presence (24:40-43). This very careful self-identification indicates the importance attached by Jesus to his acceptance by the eleven as the same person they had known as Jesus prior to his death.

This careful self-identification of Jesus is quite in harmony with the importance he always attached to his own person. His effort was ever to bring the twelve to some measure of acceptance of the exalted position he held in his own eyes. It is not simply as their friend come to life that he wishes them to recognize him now; he desires that they shall identify him as Jesus in order that they may conserve all that the person Jesus was and wished to be to them before he died. In this self-identification of Jesus we see not only the continuation of his personality but the preservation beyond death of the consciousness through which he came to know and reveal himself as the Son of God. Death did not destroy this consciousness. It was carried over beyond Calvary to become the inspiration of the belief on the part of the disciples that he was all he had claimed to be prior to the crucifixion. From the minds of the early disciples this belief was to be implanted in the minds of others, who in turn were to pass it on. Thus it becomes a part of the stream of history.

2. *Jesus interpreted his death as central in the fulfilment of God's purpose in history as revealed through Israel.* One of the chief purposes of the resurrection appearances of Jesus was to make clear the meaning of his death to his disciples. When the two who walked with him to Emmaus related to him the story of his death and the report of the empty tomb, he said to them: "Was it not necessary for the Christ to suffer these things and enter into his glory?" There follows this statement by Luke: "And beginning at Moses and all the prophets, he expounded unto them in all the scriptures the things concerning himself" (Luke 24:26 f.). After he had eaten in the presence of the eleven in Jerusalem, he said: "These are the words which I spake unto you, while I was yet with you, that all things must be fulfilled, which were written in the law of Moses, and in the prophets, and in the psalms, concerning me. Then opened he their understanding, that they might understand [go on understanding, *suneinai*—present infinitive] the scriptures. And said unto them, Thus it is written, and thus it behoved Christ to suffer and to rise from the dead the third day" (Luke 24:44-46).

There is remarkable harmony between the tone and content of these sayings of Jesus with all that his words and conduct reveal of his consciousness concerning himself prior to his death. We saw how the choice made by him in the wilderness of Judea identified him with God's redemptive purpose as manifested in his dealings with Israel. In this decision Jesus became the Servant of Jehovah whose character and mission were described in the great "Servant" passages of Isaiah. The declaration made by Jesus at Nazareth showed that he thought of himself as the Servant. The reply that he made to the question of John the Baptist indicated his fidelity to the Servant pattern. At Caesarea Philippi he accepted Peter's confession of himself as the Christ the Son of the living God and referred to himself as the Son of Man. But at Caesarea Philippi he made the great revelation of his impending death, indicating the fusion in his own mind of the Servant concept with the other great concepts of the Christ (the Messiah), the Son of God, and the Son of Man, as applying to himself. In the official presentation of himself as King Messiah to the Jewish nation he rode into the city upon an ass, revealing again his fidelity to the character of the Servant of Jehovah. In all his conduct from this point on till his death he displayed the character of the Servant, while revealing his conviction that he was the Son of God and King of Israel. There is perfect consistency in Jesus, therefore, from the beginning to the close of his ministry, a consistency that arises out of his knowledge of the character of his Father God and his identification with God's redemptive purpose as projected and progressively revealed in the Chosen People.

The chief concern of Jesus during the resurrection appearances is that the disciples shall realize all this, and come to see the significance of his death in the eternal purpose of God. He desires that the disciples shall see his death against the background of the long dealing of Jehovah with Israel. He tells them *it was necessary for the Christ to suffer—"Thus it is written."* The necessity arose out of the fidelity of the Son and Messiah in an evil world to the character of the loving God. The Son and Messiah—yes, even the great Son of Man—must be the Suffering Servant if he is to be the true representative of God the Father and the fulfiller of God's redemptive purpose as revealed in the Scriptures. Thus Jesus is careful to unfold to the disciples how Moses, the Psalms, and the prophets had spoken of him and foretold the necessity of his sufferings. He opened their mind "that they might go on comprehending [*sunienai*] the scriptures."

Whatever one's view of the resurrection may be, he must admit that the revelation of himself made by this Jesus of the Lukan resurrection narratives is in perfect harmony with the revelation which Jesus is represented as making of himself prior to his death, in the Synoptic Gospels. The resurrection narratives represent Jesus as seeing himself as the fulfiller of Old Testament prophecy and history, as the Christ who was destined to suffer that the redemptive purposes of God might be brought to fruition. In so doing they bring together in one wonderful synthesis all that Jesus conceived himself to be, under the grand formula: *"Thus it is written."*

3. *Jesus saw himself as now invested with authority to send his disciples on a mission of world conquest and worldwide proclamation of redemption from sin.* He tells the eleven in Jerusalem that it was also "written" that "repentance and remission of sins should be preached in my name among all nations, beginning at Jerusalem." He adds, "And ye are witnesses of these things" (Luke 24:47 f.). The final commission to the disciples, as given by Matthew, was: "All power is given unto me in heaven and in earth. Go ye therefore, and teach all nations, baptizing them in the name of the Father, and of the Son, and of the Holy Ghost: teaching them to observe all things whatsoever I have commanded you: and, lo, I am with you alway, even unto the end of the world" (Matthew 28:18-20).

The consciousness of Jesus of his Sonship, Messiahship, and Saviourhood reaches a grand and logical climax in this Commission to the disciples to proclaim what they have seen and heard. "All power is given unto me in heaven and in earth" is a rightful claim to be made by One who believes himself to be the unique Son of God and Redeemer of mankind. The inevitable and logical expression of such authority is a program for conquest of the world. Only the wide world is adequate as a field of conquest for him who knows himself to be the Son of the living God.

II. Jesus in History

The opinions which Jesus held concerning himself would be of some value from the standpoint of psychology. As belonging to a religious genius, or to a religious fanatic, his mind would offer a fruitful field of investigation for the student of psychology. His beliefs would also be interesting simply because they were the beliefs of one of the great men of history. But the quest we have made could not be justified on these grounds. It is necessary that the consciousness of Jesus as to his person and mission be validated in history if the quest is to be justified.

To show adequately that Jesus' estimate of himself is validated in history would require the writing of another book. It is not necessary to be so elaborate in justifying the effort we have made to determine Jesus' conception of himself. It is only necessary to present in abbreviated fashion argument for the position that history vindicates the opinion that Jesus held concerning himself. The argument follows.

1. *History provides no rival to Jesus in the character of his consciousness concerning himself.* The convictions that other great religious leaders held with reference to themselves bear little resemblance to the exalted estimate entertained by Jesus of himself and his mission. We select for comparison with Jesus the three best-known founders of other religions: Buddha, Confucius, and Mohammed. Buddha held no exalted opinion concerning himself. He certainly did not believe he was the Son of God. As a matter of fact, he discouraged belief in a supreme being and taught men to rely upon themselves rather than upon God and religion. Confucius held a very humble opinion of himself. He said: "In letters I am perhaps equal to other men. But the character of the superior man, carrying out in his conduct what he professes, is what I have not yet attained to."[1] Mohammed thought of himself as the

[1] Hume: *The World's Living Religions*, p. 113. By permission of the publishers, Charles Scribner's Sons, New York.

prophet of Allah and spoke of himself as "A man from amongst yourselves, to warn you, and that ye may fear." [2] He never claimed to be the Son of God.

The superiority of the consciousness of Jesus to that of these men is not merely in the more exalted opinions which he held concerning himself. In the consciousness of Jesus is to be found a remarkable awareness to the demands of history and an extraordinary realization of the unique place occupied by himself in the scheme of history. This is seen in his recognition of the unfolding pattern of Israel's history, of Israel's mission to the world, and of his part in the fulfilment of that mission. The founders of other religions fail to approach Jesus in this aspect of his consciousness. There is a comprehensiveness, a completeness, a satisfying inclusiveness in the consciousness of Jesus not to be found in the minds of these other religious leaders.

History validates Jesus' estimate of himself and his mission because it produces no other founder of a religion of any consequence whose consciousness or self-estimate is comparable to that of Jesus. History testifies to the uniqueness of Jesus' consciousness and to the truth of the opinions which he held about himself.

2. *History offers nothing to contradict the interpretation that Jesus made of Israel's history and of his unique place in that history.* We have seen that Jesus found himself at home in the higher prophetic stream of Israel. In this stream he saw the unfolding purpose of God to redeem humanity and bless the world through the Chosen People. He saw the Messiah as the universal Redeemer in whom this redemptive purpose was headed up, and he believed and taught that he was this Messiah. Renouncing all temporal and materialistic interpretations of the Messiah, he was convinced that he was the great Son of Man of the prophecies of Daniel and Enoch, as well as the Son of God. But again he identified himself closely with the higher prophetic stream by seeing himself as the Suffering Servant of Jehovah. In his person and mission he saw the complete

[2] *Ibid.*, p. 219.

spiritual fulfilment of all the promises in the law and the prophets concerning the Great One who was to come.

Almost twenty centuries have passed since the crucifixion of Jesus. Surely sufficient time has elapsed for history to produce a rival to Jesus in his great claims to be the Messiah of Israel and the universal Saviour, if ever it had been possible for such a rival to appear upon the scene of history. The history of the Jews since the latter part of the first century has served to confirm the claims of Jesus. In A.D. 70 the Temple was destroyed and an end was made of the theocracy. Since that time the people of Israel have been as "sheep without a shepherd." Scattered in all parts of the world, broken up into various camps, "liberals," "orthodox," rationalists, humanists, atheists, the Jews are no longer the "people called Israel." With dogged persistence many of them attempt to preserve the old ways and maintain the integrity of the "nation." But the unity that is maintained is more racial than religious and even the unity of the race is disintegrating. As a people the Jews are compelled to look backward to glory; there is little that the future holds for them as a separate people. There is nothing in Jewish history since A.D. 70 to suggest the advent of any other Messiah than Jesus, and there is nothing in that history to contradict his claim that he was the Messiah of Israel, and that as such he fulfilled Israel's mission to the world. Indeed Jewish history from the first century on confirms the claims of Jesus.

3. *History offers by contrast ample evidence of the rightness of Jesus' program for humanity.* By "program" we mean the totality of the way of life which Jesus contemplated for humanity under the divine order designated by him as the Kingdom of God, and offered to the world by him on his authority as Son of God. We have seen that Jesus freed the Kingdom concept from the strictures of the old Davidic monarchial idea and universalized it. The Kingdom Jesus taught was the universal spiritual dominion of God in humanity. This dominion was to find actualization in the lives of individuals recognizing the sovereignty of God and acting as true children of the Heavenly Father. Thus the Kingdom embraced an order in society.

Jesus conceived of this order in society as the "saving salt" of humanity. An unbiased study of the ethics of this Kingdom order must convince even the most skeptical that it is designed to provide peace, happiness, and human welfare. Obedience to the ethics of the Kingdom would abolish the major evils that now afflict society and create a new order of justice and brotherhood. History reveals the folly of humanity in not accepting the Kingdom order as the order for society. Humanity has paid and continues to pay dearly for its folly. The incessant wars that have afflicted the race, the unbridled lust for power shown by individuals and groups, the fierce competition between nations and groups for wealth, the exploitation of human beings for material gain, the indifference of privileged classes to the misery of human beings caught in the toils of poverty and disease—all of these have perpetuated the ancient social evils that have plagued the race and caused untold suffering to millions of human beings. Over against this long record of humanity's failure to provide something better is the program of Jesus, the order of Jesus, which by every known standard must be adjudged far superior to the present world order.

History has produced nothing better and gives no promise of ever producing anything as practical, as workable, or as good as that which Jesus offered to the world in the Kingdom of God. This is worthy to be classed as a testimony to the rightness of the conviction of Jesus that as the Son of God and Saviour of mankind he was invested with authority to offer to the world a new order of life in this universal Kingdom of God.

4. *In millions of cases history offers evidence of the effectiveness of Jesus' way of life for the individual,* a way based upon his authority as the Lord of life. Jesus is imperious, speaking with the authority of the Son of God, as he comes to the individual and demands of him the utter loyalty of a slave for a master, or of a subject for his sovereign, promising in return happiness and self-realization. From the time the fishermen left their boats and nets on the Galilean lake to heed his summons, to the present, men have gladly given to Jesus their complete devo-

tion. From the beginning they have been willing to suffer for him and die in his service. The lives of these who suffered and died, and the lives of countless millions who loved and served him without paying the supreme price, testify to the effectiveness of the salvation Jesus promises to the individual. Inner peace, joy, integration of personality, self-realization, adjustment to life—these have been the rewards that have come to men and women in all ages who have followed the way of Jesus. Many of these men and women have left their testimonies in written records that reveal the effectiveness of Jesus' work and validate his claim to be the Lord of life and the Saviour of men. Others have simply lived their lives as humble but effective witnesses of the power of the Son of God to give to men abundant, victorious life. History speaks in the millions of Jesus' followers, from the early days until now, and says: *"His way for the individual is right!"*

5. *History shows that any interpretation of Jesus which disregards or discounts his own interpretation of himself is incapable of sustaining any enduring and effective spiritual movement.* Adequate demonstration of this fact would require a too elaborate reference to church history, but a casual knowledge of the history of the Christian movement discloses the fact that it has been the stream which stems from the consciousness of Jesus that he was the Son of God that has sustained the Christian movement through the centuries. Heresies flourish for a time and die; some few continue to live alongside true Christianity, *but they live because of Christianity,* and what life they have they derive from that central stream of Christianity that exalts Jesus as the Christ, the Son of God. We have witnessed in our own time the decline of a "liberalism," which under the impact of modern science, surrendered the conviction that Jesus held concerning his person. This "liberalism" was extremely critical of "conservative" Christianity, but the only values it had came, in fact, from the conservative tradition—its "social gospel," for instance, which was inspired by the ethics of the Kingdom of God, had no real validation apart from the authority of Jesus as the Son of God. This "liberalism," like Unitar-

ianism, had little missionary power because of its superficial view of salvation. It also failed to provide proper climate in the churches for soul development; it lacked warmth. Confident and a bit arrogant in the heyday of the movement a few brief years ago, the leaders of this so-called "liberalism" are not nearly so vocal as they were; some have made avowed reversals of their former positions. The movement is dying for want of life. Meantime true liberalism, the liberalism which accepts both Jesus' evaluation of himself and his evaluation of man, takes on new life and gives promise of providing a leadership for the Christian movement which will open a new chapter in Christian history and in history itself.

6. *The movement of history is in the direction of universalism and the unification of mankind, and only Christianity, of all the world's living religions, is appropriate to this movement.* The point calls for little argument. One of the commonest of modern observations is the smallness of the world as a result of recent scientific advances in transportation and communication. The day draws nearer when the world will be one community. The dream of a community of nations was partially realized in the League of Nations, after World War I. There is a very definite trend toward some sort of association of nations for the preservation of peace after the present war is over. The movement toward universalism will not be impeded—it will go on—this is the lesson of history. The only religion in the world today which is adequate to this trend toward universalism is Christianity. This is true because of the character of Jesus and his gospel. Neither Buddhism nor Mohammedanism nor Confucianism—to take three of the world's leading religions—can in any way compare with Christianity in its universal appeal. Jesus presents himself to mankind as the unique Son of God and the universal Saviour. The Kingdom which he preached is based upon the sovereignty of God over all men and over all life. Through the centuries Christianity has demonstrated its universal appeal by its acceptance in all parts of the world by many races of men. Vast numbers of people have been willing to forsake their native religions be-

cause they recognized in Christianity a finality which they saw was not present in the old religions. There is in Christ as the Son of God a catholicity and a finality which can and will meet the demands of the continuing movement of history toward universalism.

7. *Jesus is the only individual in history who unifies and gives purpose to history.* This he does: (1) by rooting his claims to be the Son of God and universal Saviour in the history of Israel which begins with creation and traces a divine purpose in history through the prophetic era; (2) by making himself the bridge over which the central purpose of history passes from the prophetic era to the first century and on into the future; (3) by projecting into history a unifying, universal, and perpetual order in the Kingdom of God, an order capable of shaping and giving direction to history; (4) by providing for the consummation of history in his *Parousia.*

Thus in Jesus Christ as Son of God and in his revelation and work as the Son there is a philosophy of history. Paul saw this brilliantly when he said: "That in the dispensation of the fullness of the times he [God] might head up [*anakephalaiōsasthai*] all things in the Christ, the things in heaven and those upon the earth" (Ephesians 1:10). And so we may feel with confidence that there is logic, meaning, and purpose in history. God's hand is in history! There is a "divine event toward which the whole creation moves." And those who accept God's revelation in Jesus Christ his Son are in the central stream of history's great purpose!

In all of this history vindicates Jesus Christ in the estimate that he made of himself and of his mission. In all of this there is renewed assurance that Jesus is the hope of the world.

Jesus therefore lives beyond Calvary. He lives in history. He lives forevermore!

INDEX